Edith Wharton's
THE AGE OF
INNOCENCE

CURRENTLY AVAILABLE

The Adventures of Huckleberry Finn
Mark Twain

Aeneid
Vergil

Animal Farm
George Orwell

The Autobiography of Malcolm X
Alex Haley & Malcolm X

Beowulf

Billy Budd, Benito Cereno, & Bartleby the Scrivener
Herman Melville

Brave New World
Aldous Huxley

The Catcher in the Rye
J. D. Salinger

Crime and Punishment
Fyodor Dostoevsky

The Crucible
Arthur Miller

Death of a Salesman
Arthur Miller

The Divine Comedy (Inferno)
Dante

A Farewell to Arms
Ernest Hemingway

Frankenstein
Mary Shelley

The Grapes of Wrath
John Steinbeck

Great Expectations
Charles Dickens

The Great Gatsby
F. Scott Fitzgerald

Gulliver's Travels
Jonathan Swift

Hamlet
William Shakespeare

Heart of Darkness & The Secret Sharer
Joseph Conrad

Henry IV, Part One
William Shakespeare

I Know Why the Caged Bird Sings
Maya Angelou

Iliad
Homer

Invisible Man
Ralph Ellison

Jane Eyre
Charlotte Brontë

Julius Caesar
William Shakespeare

King Lear
William Shakespeare

Lord of the Flies
William Golding

Macbeth
William Shakespeare

A Midsummer Night's Dream
William Shakespeare

Moby-Dick
Herman Melville

Native Son
Richard Wright

Nineteen Eighty-Four
George Orwell

Odyssey
Homer

Oedipus Plays
Sophocles

Of Mice and Men
John Steinbeck

The Old Man and the Sea
Ernest Hemingway

Othello
William Shakespeare

Paradise Lost
John Milton

Pride and Prejudice
Jane Austen

The Red Badge of Courage
Stephen Crane

Romeo and Juliet
William Shakespeare

The Scarlet Letter
Nathaniel Hawthorne

Silas Marner
George Eliot

The Sun Also Rises
Ernest Hemingway

A Tale of Two Cities
Charles Dickens

Tess of the D'Urbervilles
Thomas Hardy

To Kill a Mockingbird
Harper Lee

Uncle Tom's Cabin
Harriet Beecher Stowe

Wuthering Heights
Emily Brontë

Edith Wharton's
THE AGE OF INNOCENCE

NOTES

A CONTEMPORARY
LITERARY VIEWS BOOK

Edited and with an Introduction by
HAROLD BLOOM

© 1991 by Chelsea House Publishers, a subsidiary of Haights Cross Communications.

Introduction © 1999 by Harold Bloom

Printed and bound in the United States of America.

3 5 7 9 8 6 4 2

The hardback of this edition has been cataloged as follows:

Library of Congress Cataloging-in-Publication Data

Edith Wharton's The age of innocence / edited and with an introduction by Harold Bloom.
p.   cm. — (Bloom's Notes)
"Contemporary Literary Views book."
Includes bibliographical references and index.
ISBN 0-7910-4515-3 (hbk.)— ISBN 0-7910-4918-3 (pbk.)
1. Wharton, Edith, 1862-1937. Age of innocence--Examinations–
–Study guides.   I. Bloom, Harold. II. Series.
PS3545.H16A734 1998
813'.52—dc21
98-13286
CIP

Chelsea House Publishers
1974 Sproul Road, Suite 400
Broomall, PA 19008-0914

Contents

User's Guide

This volume is designed to present biographical, critical, and bibliographical information on the author and the work. Following Harold Bloom's editor's note and introduction are a detailed biography of the author, discussing major life events and important literary works. Then follows a thematic and structural analysis of the work, which traces significant themes, patterns, and motifs. An annotated list of characters supplies brief information on the chief characters in the work.

A selection of critical extracts, derived from previously published material by leading critics, then follows. The extracts consist of statements by the author, early reviews of the work, and later evaluations up to the present. These items are arranged chronologically by date of first publication. A bibliography of the author's writings (including a complete list of all books written, cowritten, edited, and translated), a list of additional books and articles on the author and the work, and an index of themes conclude the volume.

Harold Bloom is Sterling Professor of the Humanities at Yale University and Henry W. and Albert A. Berg Professor of English at the New York University Graduate School. He is the author of twenty books and the editor of more than thirty anthologies of literary criticism.

Professor Bloom's works include *Shelley's Mythmaking* (1959), *The Visionary Company* (1961), *Blake's Apocalypse* (1963), *Yeats* (1970), *A Map of Misreading* (1975), *Kabbalah and Criticism* (1975), and *Agon: Towards a Theory of Revisionism* (1982). *The Anxiety of Influence* (1973) sets forth Professor Bloom's provocative theory of the literary relationships between the great writers and their predecessors. His most recent books include *The American Religion* (1992), *The Western Canon* (1994), and *Omens of Millennium: The Gnosis of Angels, Dreams, and Resurrection* (1996).

Professor Bloom earned his Ph.D. from Yale University in 1955 and has served on the Yale faculty since then. He is a 1985 MacArthur Foundation Award recipient and served as the Charles Elkot Norton Professor of Poetry at Harvard University in 1987–88. He is currently the editor of other Chelsea House series in literary criticism, including MAJOR LITERARY CHARACTERS, MODERN CRITICAL VIEWS, and WOMEN WRITERS OF ENGLISH AND THEIR WORKS.

Editor's Note

My introduction contrasts *The Age of Innocence* with Henry James's *praxis* as a novelist, and concludes that the differences are far greater than the similarities.

The Critical Extracts begin with Carl Van Doren's consideration of the novel as a study of the oppressions that a closed social community puts upon its constituents. Q. D. Leavis opines that Wharton's people all are archaic survivals, while Edmund Wilson compares *The Age of Innocence* to *The Europeans* of Henry James and finds the divergence striking. The artistry of *Age* is praised by Blake Nevius, while Viola Hopkins considers the book's imagery.

The novelist Louis Auchincloss, a legitimate literary heir of Wharton, endorses her tacit approval of Newland Archer's self-sacrifice, while Grace Kellogg Shaw Smith finds the novel essentially an elegy for Old New York.

In Arthur Mizener's view, both the love and the frustration of Newland Archer and Ellen Olenska are equally inevitable. Wharton's distinguished biographer, R. W. B. Lewis, catches the full poignancy of Newland and Ellen's mutual renunciation, while Gary H. Lindberg examines the narrative strategy of *The Age of Innocence*.

Margaret B. McDowall emphasizes that Archer never sees his wife May as a woman rather than a stereotype, while Cynthia Griffin Wolff explores the hidden relation between Wharton's novel and James's *The Portrait of a Lady*. The sense in which Wharton's characters are "buried alive" by their society is adumbrated by Sidney H. Bremer, and Cushing Strout returns us to the relation between Wharton and James, noting that Newland Archer is a complement to Isabel Archer.

Old New York's fear of reality is Carol Wershoven's focus, while Wendy Gimbel centers on the novel's conclusion. Susan Goodman finds May and Ellen more alike than Archer suspects, and David Holbrook intimates that Wharton surpasses James in her understanding of erotic need.

For Kathy A. Fedorko, Wharton's novel is a kind of Gothic, while Katherine Joslin concludes the Critical Extracts with acute remarks upon Newland Archer's severe limitations in all his relations to women.

Introduction

HAROLD BLOOM

A profound study of Edith Wharton's own nostalgias, *The Age of Innocence* (1920) achieved a large discerning audience immediately and has retained it since. For Wharton herself, the novel was a prelude to her autobiography, *A Backward Glance*, published 14 years later and three years before her death. Wharton, who was 57 in 1919 when *The Age of Innocence* was in most part composed, associated herself with both her protagonists, Newland Archer and Ellen Olenska. *The Age of Innocence* is a historical novel set in socially prominent Old New York of the early 1870s, a vanished world indeed when seen from a post-World War I perspective. Wrongly regarded by many critics as a novel derived from Henry James, *The Age of Innocence* is rather a deliberate complement to *The Portrait of a Lady*, seeking and finding a perspective that James was conscious of having excluded from his masterpiece. Wharton might well have called her novel *The Portrait of a Gentleman,* since Newland Archer's very name is an allusion to Isabel Archer, a far more attractive and fascinating character than Wharton's unheroic gentleman of Old New York.

Not that Newland is anything but a very decent and good man who will become a useful philanthropist and civic figure. Unfortunately, however, he has no insight whatsoever as to the differences between men and women, and his passion is of poor quality compared to Ellen's. R. W. B. Lewis, Wharton's biographer, regards *The Age of Innocence* as a minor masterpiece. Time so far has confirmed Lewis's judgment, but we now suffer through an age of ideology, and I am uncertain as to whether *The Age of Innocence* will be strong enough to endure. I have no doubts about Wharton's *The House of Mirth* and *The Custom of the Country,* but I wonder whether Newland Archer may yet sink his own book. The best historical novel of Old New York, *The Age of Innocence* retains great interest both as social history and as social anthropology. One is always startled by the farewell dinner of Ellen Olenska, where Newland realizes that he is attending "the tribal rally around a kinswoman about to be eliminated from the tribe." Wharton's own judgment, as narrator, sums up this tribal expulsion:

> It was the Old New York way of taking life "without effusion of blood": the way of people who dreaded scandal more than disease, who placed decency above courage, and who considered that nothing was more ill-bred than "scenes," except the behavior of those who gave rise to them.

That seems a condemnation of Old New York, and yet it is not. Throughout the novel, Wharton acknowledges that Newland's world centers upon an idea of order, a convention that stifles passion and yet liberates from chaos. The old order at least *was* an order; Wharton was horrified at the post-World War I United States. Newland Archer is flawed in perception: of his world, of his wife, most of all of Ellen. And yet Wharton subtly makes it clear that even a more courageous and perceptive Newland would not have made a successful match with Ellen. Their relationship in time must have dissolved, with Newland returning to the only tribe that could sustain him. Henry James's Isabel Archer, returning to her dreadful husband Osmond, also accepts an idea of order, but one in which her renunciation has a transcendental element. Wharton, shrewder if less sublime than her friend James, gives us a more realistic yet a less consequential Archer. ❖

Biography of Edith Wharton

(1862–1937)

Edith Newbold Jones was born January 24, 1862, in New York City, the third child and only daughter of George Frederic Jones and Lucretia Stevens Rhinelander. They were a wealthy family with colonial antecedents, and Edith was educated privately at home and in Europe. From an early age, she was at ease with foreign languages and the social life of England and the continent. Before she could read or write, the young Edith was an enthusiastic storyteller, interrupting her daily activities and retreating to her room to imagine elaborate fictions that she would tell aloud.

The first of her poems came to the attention of Henry Wadsworth Longfellow and were published privately in 1878. In 1883 her poems were published in *The Atlantic Monthly*. She would publish two more volumes of poetry: *Artemis to Acteon* (1909) and *Twelve Poems* (1925).

Edith married Edward Robbins Wharton, a Boston banker thirteen years her senior, in 1885. They lived successively in New York City; Newport, Rhode Island; and Lenox, Massachusetts. They traveled frequently to Europe, and in 1907 she settled permanently in France, returning to the United States only occasionally. Edith and Edward divorced in 1913, after he had embezzled her funds. In addition to Edith's lifelong friend Walter Berry, Henry James was a friend and frequent visitor during her travels and in the United States. James and Wharton traveled by car through many regions of Europe and through the countryside surrounding The Mount, her Lenox home.

A book on interior decoration, *The Decoration of Houses* (1897), published in collaboration with the architect Ogden Codman, reflected Wharton's interest in domestic architecture. In 1899, she published the best of her early tales in *The Greater Inclination*. Another collection of stories, *Crucial Instances*

(1901), was followed by Wharton's first long novel, *The Valley of Decision* (1902). Her novelette *Sanctuary* appeared in 1903, and a short story collection, *The Descent of Man*, the following year.

The House of Mirth (1905) was the first of Wharton's works to become an enduring masterpiece and is arguably her best novel. In it she describes the "tribal" social system of New York in the 1870s. Like Henry James, she elevates this study of the effects of false social values from a novel of manners to tragedy. Although Jamesian themes appear frequently in her novels, Wharton's point of view is much different: while James examined the contrast between American and European customs and character, Edith Wharton satirically explored—from a female point of view—the changes in New York society during her lifetime.

The concerns of the rich and of characters in conflict with their society continued to be themes in Wharton's work during most of her career. Her most significant novels include *Ethan Frome* (1911), *The Reef* (1912), and *Summer* (1917). During this period she also published *The Custom of the Country* (1913), an international novel of manners featuring an American social climber in France, and three more collections of short stories: *The Hermit and the Wild Woman and Other Stories* (1908), *Tales of Men and Ghosts* (1910), and *Xingu and Other Stories* (1916).

Wharton was active in organizing national relief projects in France during World War I, and in 1916 she was awarded the Cross of the Legion of Honor by the French government. *Fighting France, from Dunkerque to Belfort* (1915), *The Marne* (1918), and *A Son at the Front* (1923) came out of her wartime experiences.

The Age of Innocence, published in 1920, received the Pulitzer Prize the following year. Henry James's continuing influence on Wharton is revealed in the novel's single-character perspective and its ironic treatment of New York high society. *Old New York* (1924), Wharton's collection of four novelettes about New York in the second half of the 19th century, includes *False Dawn; The Old Maid*, which was rejected for publication many times but received the 1935 Pulitzer Prize as a stage adaptation by Zoe

Akins; *The Spark,* an extraordinary tale of Walt Whitman's influence on a chance acquaintance; and *New Year's Day.* Three of Wharton's subsequent novels focused upon the relations of parents and children: *The Mother's Recompense* (1925); *The Twilight Sleep,* a 1927 best-seller; and *The Children* (1928).

In 1925, Wharton published a work of literary criticism, *The Writing of Fiction* (1925), in which she analyzed her own story-telling process. In her discussions about characters' names, inexhaustible sources of subject matter, and the occult nature of literary inspiration, the author provided insight both into her works and into those of other writers of her literary generation. Her task as a fiction writer, she believed, was to find the human significance of a story; she relates that her characters would reveal themselves to her as she created them.

Hudson River Bracketed (1929) is the most ambitious of her later novels. In this work and in its sequel, *The Gods Arrive* (1932), Wharton compares European cultures to those of certain regions in the United States. Her last novels were *Here and Beyond* (1926), *Certain People* (1930), *Human Nature* (1933), *The World Over* (1936), and *Ghosts,* published in 1937, the year of her death. An unfinished novel, *The Buccaneers,* was published posthumously in 1938.

In her 1934 autobiography, *A Backward Glance,* Wharton tells of the pleasures of childhood reading, the hesitancy of the young writer, and the singular joys of travel and friendship. Among her friends and acquaintances were many influential figures, including Charles Eliot Norton, Thomas Hardy, H. G. Wells, Andre Gide, and the exuberant young writer Jean Cocteau. Edith Wharton died on August 11, 1937, at Pavillon Colombe, her home in St. Brice-sous-Foret, France. She is buried at the Cimetiere des Gonards at Versailles, near the grave of her friend Walter Berry. ✤

Thematic and Structural Analysis

"On a January evening of the early seventies, Christine Nilsson was singing in *Faust* at the Academy of Music in New York." Marking this performance (**book one, chapter one**), *The Age of Innocence* immediately invokes a time, a place, and a particular social and high-cultural milieu. The degree to which social strictures become private behavior is the novel's focus. The defeat of individual freedom by social forces is the novel's theme. Details of everyday life permeate the text: with "a playful allusion to democratic principals," the seemingly more reckless of the opera-goers embrace the novelty of the hired carriage, prototype of the taxicab. The narrator is a bemused observer, privy to gossip and character and not wholly unsympathetic to the "totem terrors" of nineteenth-century New York society.

Newland Archer, a character in some ways reminiscent of the young Edith Wharton herself, carefully observes social propriety. He draws a "breath of satisfied vanity" as he gazes upon May Welland, seated in the Mingott family opera box with her mother and grandmother, Mrs. Lovell Mingott. May holds an enormous bouquet of lilies-of-the-valley that Archer has sent to her. She appears artlessly captivated by the romantic action on the stage, blushing attractively and lightly touching the flowers. Newland feels a "thrill of possessorship in which pride in his own masculine initiation was mingled with a tender reverence for her abysmal purity." Their engagement is due to be announced soon, and he contemplates a honeymoon during which he will educate her, achieving at last that "miracle of fire and ice" which will yield a wife of tact, wit, and an eagerness to please him in all things.

Seated with Newland in the club box, Lawrence Lefferts is respected among the bachelors as "the foremost authority on 'form' in New York." He peruses the audience and is shocked by the arrival of another woman to the Mingott box. Sillerton Jackson, the authority on "family," who has "between his narrow hollow temples" a 50-year log of New York society scandals and gossip, remarks mildly upon the family's audacity: "I didn't think the Mingotts would have tried it on."

Newland Archer is caught between the risk of "bad form" and the proper loyalty to May Welland and, by extension, her family (**chapter two**). Countess Ellen Olenska, May's cousin and also a granddaughter of Mrs. Mingott, is the notorious object of attention of "masculine New York." Having left her husband, who is reportedly "a brute," Lefferts informs them, "she bolted with his secretary." Newland admires the Mingott's "resolute championship of the few black sheep that their blameless stock had produced," yet he is appalled by their publicly placing the disgraced cousin beside the young girl whose engagement to him will be announced within a few weeks. As a narrative technique, Archer's limited perspective works in two ways: Wharton fictionalizes and distances her autobiographical recollections, and she establishes Archer's character. Henry James uses a similar technique of psychological development in his novels.

Newland muses upon the powerful social position and public character of Catherine (Mrs. Manson) Mingott, the family matriarch, as the narrative reminds us that the American aristocracy has sprung from various and unaristocratic beginnings. The "visible proof of her moral courage" is her house, built in the "wilderness" near Central Park, at the "frontier above the Forties." All this, however, does not diminish the gravity of the situation in which May Welland is caught. He is disturbed by the presence of Ellen Olenska: "Few things seemed to Newland Archer more awful than an offense against 'Taste,'" and "the way [Ellen's] dress (which had no tucker) sloped away from her thin shoulders shocked and troubled him."

At the end of the opera's first act, Newland and May begin another sort of public performance. He enters the Mingott box to sit beside May in a display of support which they both know to be a social necessity. Newland wants May to tell Madame Olenska that they are engaged and to announce it publicly at a ball to be held later that evening. "Tell your cousin yourself: I give you leave," she answers, moving her chair so that Newland may sit beside the Countess Olenska. Wharton presents

Ellen as one accused and the opera audience the tribunal that will decide her fate. To Ellen, as her conversation with Newland makes clear, this tribunal is a thing to be met, at least privately, with genteel derision. She dryly posits that she must be dead and that New York society is heaven. Archer is intrigued, but not amused. He does not mention his engagement.

The **third chapter** introduces Mr. and Mrs. Julius Beaufort. Regina Beaufort had been a "penniless beauty" from an "honorable" family, but mystery surrounds her husband. "The question was: who *was* [Julius] Beaufort?" the narrator asks. An annual ball, held after this opera performance, is the most persuasive testament to their social superiority, for theirs is one of the few homes in New York to possess a ballroom. At the Beauforts', awaiting the arrival of the Mingott party, Archer worries that the Mingotts may bring the Countess Olenska. The disapproval of his fellows in the club box of the theater has shaken his chivalrous resolve to publicly support May's cousin. May announces their engagement that evening, and Archer feigns disappointment that Ellen has decided not to attend the ball after all.

As part of the engagement ritual, Newland and May visit Mrs. Manson Mingott to receive her blessing (**chapter four**). A huge woman, she is "vast and august as a natural phenomenon." Her independence from New York proprieties is marked by the unusual arrangement and purposes of the rooms in her house. Unable to climb stairs, Catherine Mingott has situated her reception rooms upstairs, while her bedroom is shockingly visible through the ground-floor sitting-room doorway. Like a scene from French fiction, such "architectural incentives to immorality" would be considered wicked, except that the old woman is and always has been irreproachable. Archer muses that, if Catherine Mingott had wanted a lover, she would have had one. His admiration for imaginary indiscretions contrasts with his relief that Ellen Olenska is not at home.

As the Archers and Wellands are leaving Catherine Mingott's home, Ellen arrives in the company of Julius Beaufort. Mrs. Mingott and Beaufort begin to gossip intimately. The "carnivorous old lady" wants information about Mrs. Lemuel Struthers, a social newcomer invited to the Beauforts' ball. Like it or not, says Mrs. Mingott, "new blood and new money" are always needed in the "tight little citadel of New York." Archer considers the impropriety of Ellen, who has just left her husband, being seen with Beaufort, and concludes that her European background makes her vulnerable to certain weaknesses. "And, in spite of the cosmopolitan views on which he prided himself," the narrator comments, Newland "thanked heaven that he was a New Yorker, and about to ally himself with one of his own kind."

Sillerton Jackson dines with the Archers in **chapter five**. Newland, his widowed mother, and his unmarried sister, Janey, emerge in their social context as Wharton probes aspects of their personal and family psychology. As with the Beauforts and Mrs. Mingott, the architecture and arrangement of their home reflects their position in the social scheme: Newland has an entire upper floor for his own use, while the women have "squeezed themselves into narrower quarters below." Sillerton Jackson likes to dine with these women not for the food, which is horrible, but for their uncritical and eager interest in gossip, especially about Ellen Olenska. The conversation would be more free, however, if Newland were absent. Newland asks why Ellen should be an outcast for having left a bad marriage. Later, alone with Sillerton Jackson, Newland claims to be "sick of the hypocrisy that would bury alive a woman of her age. . . . Women ought to be free—as free as we are," he declares, "making a discovery of which he was too irritated to measure the terrific consequences."

That evening, alone in his study (**chapter six**), Archer sees in a photograph of May that "terrifying product of the social system he belonged to and believed in, the young girl who knew nothing and expected everything." One lesson of Ellen's life is that marriage is not the "safe anchorage" he has believed. He realizes the hypocrisy of his generous-sounding words to Jackson, and considers that May's guilelessness and innocence are "cunningly manufactured by a conspiracy of mothers and aunts and grandmothers and long-dead ancestresses, because it was supposed to be what he wanted, what he had a right to." The "uncomfortable persistence and precision" of these thoughts, he realizes, are "due to the inopportune arrival of the Countess Olenska."

Chapter six concludes with an invitation from the Lovell Mingotts to a formal dinner held specifically for guests "to meet the Countess Olenska." But two days later, "the unbelievable" has occurred: almost everyone has refused the invitation. Newland's mother makes an appeal on behalf of May Welland's cousin, soon to be related to her son. She approaches Louisa van der Luyden, one of the few New Yorkers who can claim any sort of direct aristocratic ancestry and the last word on questions of social propriety. Mrs. Archer asks her son to accompany her, because "if we don't all stand together, there'll be no such thing as Society left."

The comment of Mrs. Mingott to Julius Beaufort that society needs "new blood" gains greater resonance as **chapter seven** unfolds. While his mother tells the van der Luydens "the monstrous tale of the affront inflicted on Mrs. Lovell Mingott," Newland observes that Louisa van der Luyden appears as if "gruesomely preserved in the airless atmosphere of a perfectly irreproachable existence." The van der Luydens decide to support "on principle" the Mingotts' decision to stand behind Ellen. They propose inviting the Countess Olenska to a reception at their home in honor of a visiting European duke. The invitation is later delivered to Catherine Mingott's door, and all New York society is effectively rebuked.

In **chapter eight**, Archer watches Ellen enter the van der Luyden's drawing room where "New York's most chosen company was somewhat awfully assembled." Their after-dinner conversation reveals one of the novel's peculiar ironies. Ellen expresses delight that Archer and May's engagement was not "arranged," and she is embarrassed when Newland reminds her that such marriages are not customary in America. "I don't always remember that everything here is good that was—that was bad where I've come from," she concedes. In a sense, however, Archer and May's marriage has been most carefully arranged. As May enters the crowded room, Ellen invites Archer to visit her the next day and then moves off to be introduced to other guests. Newland does not mention the invitation to May.

While waiting for the countess in the firelit drawing room of her modest home (**chapter nine,**) Archer is "bewildered" by the "Italian-looking pictures in old frames . . . like nothing he was accustomed to look at" nor therefore, the narrator adds, "able to see." Later, he tells Ellen that she has opened his eyes to "things [he'd] looked at so long that [he'd] ceased to see them." She weeps as she describes her loneliness among these "kind people" of New York society who won't allow her to voice her feelings. Overwhelmed with sympathy, Newland familiarly calls her "Ellen"—twice, he realizes, with some shock. The narrator describes his growing anxiety over his new and strange emotions: "Far down the inverted telescope he saw the faint white figure of May Welland—in New York." As he departs, he remembers that he has not sent May her daily box of lilies-of-the-valley and goes to his florist to arrange for their delivery. A "sudden revulsion of mood" overtakes him, and he sends a box of yellow roses to Ellen as well. At the last moment, he removes his signed card from the box of roses.

The next afternoon (**chapter ten**), Archer tells May that he sent roses to her cousin. "Was that right?" he asks her. She admires his thoughtfulness but remarks that Ellen, with whom she had lunch that day, never mentioned having received flowers from him. As they discuss their engagement, Archer recalls his assertion that women "ought to be as free as we are," and muses that his marriage to May will allow him to remove "the bandage" from her eyes and make her see the world as it really is. But in the same moment, he recalls having heard of a species of fish that "had ceased to develop eyes because it had no use for them." What would happen, he asks himself, if May's uncovered eyes "could only look out blankly at blankness?"

In the **eleventh chapter**, Archer, in his capacity as a lawyer, unwillingly agrees to help deter Ellen from formally divorcing her husband. The complex machinery of New York society is already acting upon the matter of the Countess Olenska. The Mingotts urge Ellen to return to her husband, but Newland argues that she is entitled to her freedom. That Archer is the agent designated to urge her not to divorce supports the novel's most powerful irony, for she will ultimately do as he asks, closing off all chances for him to escape his own life and be with her.

Archer once more enters Ellen's house in **chapter twelve**, and he is "once more conscious of the curious way in which she reversed his values, and of the need of thinking himself into conditions incredibly different from any that he knew if he were to be of use in her present difficulty." He warns Ellen that, while the laws favor divorce in her circumstance, the social customs of New York will pit the community against her. "But my freedom—is that nothing?" she asks. "It's my business, you know . . . to help you to see these things as the people who are fondest of you see them." Suddenly and resignedly, she agrees to do as he asks.

Ten days later, while attending the opera (**chapter thirteen**), Archer is reminded—"he could not have said why"—of his last parting from Ellen. The "dumb sorrow" of the lovers' parting on stage moves him greatly. He discovers that Ellen has also attended the performance, and when she sees him, she asks whether the young lover on stage will send his beloved "a bunch of yellow roses tomorrow morning." The Wellands have gone to St. Augustine for the winter, and Ellen asks what he will do while May is away. May has written to Newland, urging him to "be kind" to Ellen while she is away.

The next morning (**chapter fourteen**) Archer sends a note to the countess asking if he may visit that afternoon. He does not hear from her until three days later, when she responds from the van der Luyden's estate at Skuytercliff. "I ran away," the letter begins, "to be quiet, and think things over." He remembers that the Reggie Chiverses, whose invitation for that weekend he had recently refused, live near Skuytercliff, and sends a telegram advising them that he will be their guest, after all.

At Skuytercliff (**chapter fifteen**), Archer tells Ellen that he has come to "see what [she is] running away from," to know what has happened. "Does anything ever happen in heaven?" she responds. They go to the small house once owned by the original patroon, or proprietor, of the estate, "its panels and brasses shining in the firelight, as if magically created to receive them," and their conversation becomes more intimate in the charm of their seclusion. While they are together, however, Beaufort arrives on the pretense of having found a place for Ellen to live. It becomes clear to Archer that Beaufort is pursuing Ellen, and he weighs his chances of winning her over against Beaufort. That night, he returns to New York where, for the next few days, the "taste of the usual was like cinders in his mouth, and there were moments when he felt as if he were being buried alive under his future." Three days later, he receives a note from Ellen asking him to meet her the next day. After considering several responses, Newland decides to leave for St. Augustine to see May.

"Here was truth, here was reality, here was the life that belonged to him," the narrator remarks as Newland meets May in St. Augustine (**chapter sixteen**). Archer stays with the Wellands for a week. One day, while May and her father are out, Mrs. Welland brings up the subject of Countess Olenska's divorce, remarking that Ellen has been thoroughly "Europeanised," and thus her idea that Americans would approve of divorce particularly offensive: "That is just like the extraordinary things that foreigners invent about us. They think we dine at two o'clock and countenance divorce!" she exclaims.

Later in the week, Newland impulsively suggests to May that they marry within a few weeks. She shrewdly conjectures that his motive for urging the early wedding is his attachment to another woman, and in a poignant scene, asserts that she will sacrifice him if he has a great obligation to love and honor someone else. Newland, "full of a new awe" for his fiancée and overwhelmed by her "courage and initiative," capitulates, denying that he loves anyone but her.

Newland returns to New York to learn that Ellen has visited his mother and sister in his absence (**chapter seventeen**). "She said she wanted to know us because you'd been so good to her," Janey explains. A few days later, he calls on Catherine Mingott to deliver messages from the Wellands. With "the casual irrelevance of old age" she asks, "Now, why in the world didn't you marry my little Ellen?"

Claiming that he "wasn't made for long engagements," Archer presses her to use her influence with the Wellands to hasten his marriage to May. At that moment, Ellen walks in, and she learns that Archer has asked to move up his wedding date. As she walks him to the door, he arranges to meet with her again the following evening.

Archer arrives late at Ellen's house—half hoping that she has already gone out—and is surprised to find that she has guests. Among them is Medora Manson, who asks Archer if he will help persuade Ellen to return to her remorseful and "adoring" husband. "I would rather see her dead!" he exclaims. Medora describes the material riches and social status that Ellen would give up by divorcing, and reminds Newland that "marriage is marriage . . . and my niece is still a wife. . . ."

Ellen interrupts their conversation in **chapter eighteen**. After Medora Manson and the other guests leave, Newland asks Ellen in desperation if she intends to return to her husband. She turns the conversation to his impending marriage, asking why he is unable to convince May to marry early. "She thinks my impatience a bad sign," he admits, adding, "She thinks, in short I want to marry her at once to get away from some one that I—care for more." He confesses that she is the woman he "would have married if it had been possible" for either of them. They kiss, briefly, but when he suggests leaving May for her, Ellen lashes out at him, explaining that she agreed not to divorce her husband because he asked her to. "[Y]ou hated happiness bought by disloyalty and cruelty and indifference," she says. "That was what I'd never known before—and it's better than anything I've known." A telegram arrives for Ellen. It is from May, who announces that she will marry quickly, as Newland wishes. "Am too happy for words and love you dearly. Your grateful May," the message concludes.

In **book two, chapter nineteen**, Newland and May are married. Newland goes through the ceremony and the wedding-breakfast in a daze, warmed only faintly by May's radiance. "How like a first night at the Opera!" he muses, "recognizing all the same faces in the same boxes (no, pews), and wondering if, when the Last Trump sounded . . . whether suitable proscenium seats were already prepared for them in another world." The newlyweds embark on their honeymoon at an estate near Skuytercliff. On the way, May mentions Ellen, who claimed illness in not attending the wedding. Archer wonders if his "carefully built-up world" will always seem in danger of falling around him when he hears that name. As if part of some greater plan of May's, they stay at the patroon's house at Skuytercliff, where Newland and Ellen spent an afternoon the previous winter. Ellen, May informs her new husband, had deemed it the only house in America "that she could imagine being perfectly happy in."

In **chapter twenty** the Archers are in London, on their way home from a wedding tour. By now, Newland "had reverted to all his old inherited ideas about marriage," the narrator comments. "It was less trouble to conform with the tradition and treat May exactly as all his friends treated their wives than to try to put into practice the theories with which his untrammeled bachelorhood had dallied. There was no use in trying to emancipate a wife who had not the dimmest notion that she was not free." At a dinner party, Archer is drawn to a talented man named Monsieur Rivière, who asks Newland whether there are opportunities for him in New York: "is not the intellectual life more active there?" he inquires. Later, Archer mentions the encounter to May and she responds with mild derision: "People don't have French tutors: what does he want to do?" Newland realizes that the man would have no place in New York "as he knew it."

By the following August, at Newport, Archer has resumed his old life of routine (**chapter twenty-one**). "The idea that he could ever, in his senses, have dreamed of marrying the Countess Olenska had become almost unthinkable, and she remained in his memory simply as the most plaintive and poignant of a line of ghosts." Still, the animated party he attends at the Beauforts' Newport home "shock[s] him as if they had been children playing in a graveyard."

Having returned with May to the Welland family's vacation villa, Archer is struck by the "chain of tyrannical trifles binding one hour to the next," making "any less systematized and affluent existence seem unreal and precarious." He and May visit Catherine Mingott at her summer home, where they learn that Ellen is visiting. The old woman sends Archer to "fetch" her down at the shoreline. Archer approaches Ellen from the path leading to the water, but remains at a distance and returns to the house without speaking to her. The life that Newland is expected to lead has become "unreal and irrelevant" to him. In contrast, simply to have seen Ellen standing by the shore seems "as close to him as the blood in his veins."

In **chapter twenty-two**, Archer learns that Ellen has left Newport for a brief trip to Boston. He pretends to have business there and arrives by train the next morning (**chapter twenty-three**). Ellen is startled to see him. She has come to meet with an emissary from her husband who has offered "a considerable price" to reclaim her as his wife, an offer she has refused. She asks Archer why he did not speak to her at the beach that day at Mrs. Mingott's. "I swore I wouldn't unless you looked round," he replies. "But I didn't look round on purpose," Ellen says.

In a private dining room at an inn (**chapter twenty-four**), Archer reminds Ellen that he is "the man who married one woman because another one told him to." She counters that they must both think of May now and protect her from "disillusionment and misery." But Archer wants to keep Ellen close to him somehow. She will stay, she tells him, as long as they do not act upon their love for each other. Although they never touch during this meeting, "for a man sick with unsatisfied love, and parting for an indefinite period from the object of his passion, he felt himself almost humiliatingly calm and comforted" (**chapter twenty-five**).

Newland returns to New York by train the next morning, and is surprised to encounter Rivière, the man he had met in London. Rivière is the emissary sent by Count Olenski to deliver a message to Ellen. He has already spoken with other members of Archer's family and the Mingott families, and all are in agreement that Ellen should return to her husband. Newland realizes that he has been excluded from these negotiations, as though "some deep tribal instinct" had warned them that he could no longer be trusted in this matter. It is an epiphany for Newland, a sudden revelation of a power he has underestimated. The reader is left to guess whether Rivière is the secretary with whom Ellen is reputed to have run away from her husband. That he is more honorable than the gossip suggests underscores the nature of gossip itself.

In **chapter twenty-six** Newland's mother and Miss Sophy Jackson, Sillerton Jackson's sister, begin what is referred to as their annual examination of New York society, tracing "each new crack in its surface, and all the strange weeds pushing up between the ordered rows of social vegetables." It is Thanksgiving Day, and even the morning sermon by Dr. Ashmore portends the advent of a new societal "trend." To Mrs. Archer, "it was terrifying and yet fascinating to feel herself part of a community that was trending." As evidence of such decay, Mrs. Archer's dinner guests discuss the changes in fashion, Julius Beaufort's financial difficulties, and the new custom of attending parties on Sunday evenings, especially at the home of Mrs. Struthers, a newcomer to New York society.

The topic turns to Ellen Olenska, who had taken the unorthodox step of being the "first person to countenance" Mrs. Struthers by attending her gatherings. That Ellen had also refused to return to her husband had "surprised and inconvenienced" her family. Unable to bend her to their will, they had simply "let poor Ellen find her own level" of society, which was "in the dim depths where . . . 'people who wrote' celebrated their untidy rites."

The conversation moves to other topics, but Archer's thoughts remain on Ellen, whom he has not seen in four months. She now lives in Washington with her aunt, Medora Manson. He had written to her during those months, asking when they might meet. "Not yet," was her reply. Later, while speaking with Mr. Jackson, he becomes angry at Jackson's implication that Ellen is receiving financial assistance from Julius Beaufort and may lose it should his business fail. Archer soon realizes that his reaction has given away the fact that he has not been privy to the decisions made about Ellen on the part of his wife's family.

After Archer and May return home, Archer watches May adjust the oil lamp in his study and thinks, with horror, "How young she is! For what endless years this life will have to go on!" He tells her that he must go to Washington on business for a few days. May's response—that the trip will do him good and that he must visit Ellen—do not betray her thoughts, which Wharton describes at length: "I offer you this [hint]," May thinks, "in the only form in which well-bred people of our kind can communicate unpleasant things to each other: by letting you understand that I know you mean to see Ellen . . . and are perhaps going there expressly for that purpose . . . I wish you to do so with my full and explicit approval."

In **chapter twenty-seven**, a crisis occurs that thwarts Archer's plans to travel to Washington. The business irregularities of Julius Beaufort have culminated in the collapse of the bank and the worst financial disaster New York has yet seen. Regina Beaufort visits Catherine Mingott to beg her for support for herself and Julius; immediately after her visit, Mrs. Mingott suffers a stroke. May sends word to Newland to join the family at Catherine Mingott's home. The old woman orders that Ellen Olenska be sent for immediately. Ellen replies that she will arrive at the Jersey City train terminus the next evening (**chapter twenty-eight**). The Wellands lament the inconvenience of picking up Ellen from such a distance, and Archer offers his services. After Archer meets Ellen in May's carriage, the narrator says, "it all happened as he had dreamed" (**chapter twenty-nine**). He tells Ellen that he'd planned to travel to Washington to see her, and tries to explain the curious feeling he has each time he encounters her: "Do you know—I hardly remembered you? . . . *Each time you happen to me all over again.*" To his high-flown dreams of their being together finally "coming true," Ellen responds to him that they must look "not at visions, but at realities." Greatly disturbed, Archer gets out of the carriage and walks home, instructing the driver to continue to old Mrs. Mingott's home.

That evening in Archer's home (**chapter thirty**), May reports that her grandmother is improving. Newland finds it vaguely ominous that their conversation includes no mention of Ellen. He is further dismayed to realize that, now that May has achieved the marriage she wanted, she is "ripening into a copy of her mother, and mysteriously, by the very process, trying to turn him into a Mr. Welland." He opens a window in the room and leans out to get air.

A week later, Catherine Mingott asks to see him. He goes alone, hoping for a private moment with Ellen. The old woman announces that Ellen will be staying with her as her nurse, and requests that Newland defend Ellen's decision to the family. No matter what the rest of the family thinks, Catherine will not allow her granddaughter to be shut up in "that cage" of a marriage, she asserts. At this point, the narrator reveals that Archer had determined to run away to Washington and persuade Ellen to escape with him. With Catherine Mingott's news, he feels that Ellen has decided to stay with her grandmother to be nearer to him. It is a half-measure, but he feels "the involuntary relief of a man who has been ready to risk everything, and suddenly tastes the dangerous sweetness of security."

In **chapter thirty-one** Newland weighs the claims upon him of his marriage and of his passion for Ellen Olenska: "[F]or the first time Archer found himself face to face with the dread argument of the individual case. Ellen Olenska was like no other woman, he was like no other man: their situation, therefore, resembled no one else's, and they were answerable to no tribunal but that of their own judgment." Having learned that Ellen is visiting Regina Beaufort, he waits outside the Beaufort home to see her, and arranges a meeting for the following afternoon in the art museum.

When they meet the next day—significantly, in the antiquities gallery, filled with "small broken objects—hardly recognisable domestic . . . and personal trifles"—he asks Ellen whether she believes she will be any safer from loving him if she lives with her grandmother. "Safer from doing irreparable harm," she explains. "Don't let us be like all the others!" Before they part, she nearly gives in, quietly asking Archer "Shall I—once, come to you; and then go home?" Though tempted to say yes, Archer is taken by her "passionate honesty" and concedes that he cannot ask her to let herself be drawn "into that familiar trap." As they part, he notes her "inner radiance" that he interprets, with awe, as "love visible."

Archer returns to an empty house. May arrives home some time later, and with "an unnatural vividness," tells him that she met Ellen at Granny Mingott's. She believes she has judged Ellen unfairly, she tells her husband, but that the two cousins had had "a really good talk."

The next evening, Newland and May attend a dinner at the van der Luydens' (**chapter thirty-two**). The redoubtable couple has returned from Skuytercliff to reestablish the social order—Mrs. Lemuel Struthers cannot be allowed to usurp the social position vacated by Regina Beaufort. Ellen is not invited to the dinner, and there is much discussion about the disgrace of her having "kept her grandmother's carriage at a defaulter's door."

After dining, the party attends the same opera performance during which Archer first met Ellen two years earlier. He recalls May's words to him in St. Augustine, that she could not accept "happiness made out of a wrong—a wrong to someone else," and feels an "uncontrollable longing" to "ask [May] for the freedom he had once refused." The Archers leave the opera early on the pretense of Newland's being ill. At home, he begins what he intends to be a confession to May, saying "Madame Olenska." But before he can finish, she silences him by asking why they should discuss her cousin. "But what does it matter," she says, "now it's all over?" She informs Archer that Ellen has decided to return to Europe.

Chapter thirty-three marks the end of Newland Archer's innocence regarding the benignity of his family, his circle of friends, and the society in which he has been raised. The scene of his enlightenment is his and May's first formal dinner as a married couple. May has insisted that the occasion will be a going-away party for the Countess Olenska. As they take their seats around the table, Archer silently acknowledges that "[t]here were certain things that had to be done, and if done at all, done handsomely and thoroughly; and one of these, in the old New York code, was the tribal rally around a kinswoman about to be eliminated from the tribe. . . . It was the old New York way of taking life 'without effusion of blood.'" He is unable to say goodbye to Ellen in private; the van der Luydens have offered to drive her home.

After their guests have gone, Newland tells May that he would like to travel—"to make a break. . . . away from everything." She interrupts him with news that she is pregnant. She admits that the purpose of her conversation with Ellen at Mrs. Mingott's two weeks earlier (**chapter thirty-one**) had been to tell her first: "'I wasn't sure then—but I told her I was. And you see I was right!' she exclaimed, her blue eyes wet with victory."

The conclusion of *The Age of Innocence* (**chapter thirty-four**) takes place nearly 30 years after the events of the previous chapters. May has been dead for two years, having contracted pneumonia some time after the birth of their third child; the other children are grown; the world has changed. Newland is considered "a good citizen," a well-respected philanthropist and well-loved father; and "what was called a faithful husband." He sincerely misses his wife and "honour[s] his own past." The memory of Ellen Olenska has kept him from desiring other women, and he has "found himself held fast by habit, by memories, by a sudden startled shrinking from new things."

Nevertheless, Archer accompanies his son Dallas on a trip to Europe. In Paris, Newland realizes that he is "a mere gray speck of a man compared with the ruthless magnificent fellow he had dreamed of being." Informed by Dallas that the Countess Olenska is expecting them for a visit, Newland imagines his son for a moment possessed of old Catherine Mingott's gleeful malice. Dallas asks his father what Countess Olenska had been like. "Wasn't she . . . the woman you'd have chucked everything for, only you didn't[?]" he asks. Dallas tells Archer that May had once told him that his father "had given up the thing [he] most wanted" when she had asked him to. Moved because it was his wife, after all, who had been the one to guess his loss, Archer answers, "She never asked me."

Newland waits outside as his son enters the building where Ellen lives. He looks up at her awninged balcony and imagines her holding out her hand to him. "'It's more real to me here than if I went up,' he suddenly heard himself say." A light shines through her windows, and then a servant draws up the awning on her balcony and closes the shutters. "[A]s if it had been the signal he waited for," Newland rises from the bench and returns alone to his hotel.

Wharton's unsentimental reminiscence of love and loss is, in a sense, the record of a vanished, isolated tribe. It marks a rarefied place in American culture, where the most potent signs are not words, but customs and habits.❖

—*Tenley Williams*
New York University

List of Characters

Newland Archer is a young lawyer who marries the debutante May Welland. He struggles with a choice between individual freedom and the "tribal" demands of New York high society. In Newland's eyes, social proprieties are natural and their observance a duty. Nonetheless, he is drawn to the possibilities of a life unbound by narrow conventions, with Ellen Olenska. Though he remains with May, his passion for Ellen endures as a memory of "something he knew he had missed: the flower of life."

May Welland embodies the subtle and powerful social forces that determine Newland's choice. In her early twenties she appears, as she will all her life, as innocent and guileless as a very young girl. Her perception of Newland's love for Ellen is acute, however, and by telling Ellen she is pregnant, she convinces her to return to Europe rather than remain in New York.

Countess Ellen Olenska is May's cousin and Catherine Mingott's granddaughter. Ellen has spent most of her life in Europe. After leaving her husband, a rich Polish count, and returning to New York to live with her grandmother, she achieves "a kind of sulphurous apotheosis" among New York society gossips. For Newland, Ellen represents the world of freedom and possibility outside his own insular social circle. For New York society, Ellen is, ultimately, a disruption and a scandal.

Mrs. Manson Mingott, widowed at age twenty-eight, is the former Catherine Spicer of Staten Island, who has traveled widely in Europe and is on familiar terms with aristocrats, diplomats, artists, and even "Papists." She has a reputation both for public audacity and private irreproachability. She champions Ellen among her relatives, and supports her granddaughter financially when she returns to Europe. Monstrously obese, she rarely leaves her home.

Mrs. Archer and *Janey Archer* are Newland's mother and sister, respectively. They are a domestically active pair who grow ferns, make lace, read novels, and love gossip. They appear "as like as sisters," except that Mrs. Archer has grown stout while her unmarried daughter's dark poplins hang "more and more slackly on her virgin frame." Sharing the same habits and vocabulary, they differ only in the mother's unimaginativeness and daughter's occasional "aberrations of fancy" that rise "from springs of suppressed romance." They love Newland, and he is devoted to them.

Lawrence Lefferts is the last word on "good taste," as well as a ubiquitous conduit of gossip about Ellen Olenska. Although Lefferts himself is the object of considerable talk because of his marital infidelities, his actions are tolerated because of his gender and social status.

Sillerton Jackson is New York society's authority on "family," holding "between his narrow hollow temples" a fifty-year log of New York society scandals and gossip.

Julius and *Regina Beaufort* are society's "pet common people," as Newland's mother describes them. They are suspected to be worse than that. Wealthy and ostentatious, they possess the only formal ballroom in New York—and no one refuses their sumptuous hospitality. Beaufort's antecedents are unknown, and he is rumored to have been forced to leave England because of shady business practices. His business irregularities cause the worst financial scandal New York has ever known.

Medora Manson is Ellen's aunt and childhood guardian. "Repeatedly widowed," with ever diminishing resources, she settles into a less expensive house each time she returns to New York to recover from her travels. New York indulges Medora in her eccentricities of marriage, travel, and dress because she is born into society.

Henry and *Louisa van der Luyden* are descendants of pre-Revolutionary European aristocrats. The last representatives of an illustrious clan, they have "faded into a kind of super-terrestrial twilight." Rarely seen in public, together they are the oracle, the prophetic social authority. They preside over society in their Hudson River estate and occasionally at a "solemn house" on Madison Avenue where few guests are admitted.

Ned Winsett, Newland Archer's friend, is a journalist and failed literary critic. Archer likes Winsett for his depth of mind and his "flashes of penetration" or insight into Archer's world. He is puzzled by what he sees as Winsett's acceptance of failure and by his "savage abhorrence of social observances." Ned is a symbol of the risks inherent in adopting a "Bohemian" way of life.

Mrs. Lemuel Struthers represents the newcomers to New York society, whose wealth comes from decidedly unmysterious sources. In this case, the widow and heir to a shoe polish fortune becomes a popular hostess, despite the disdain of older, more established families.

Critical Views

CARL VAN DOREN ON THE SOCIAL FORMALISM REPRESENTED IN THE *AGE OF INNOCENCE*

[Carl Van Doren (1885–1950) was an educator, editor, and author, who taught English and rhetoric at Columbia University. He was the literary editor of the journals *Nation* and *Century*. In 1938 he was awarded a Pulitzer Prize for his biography of Benjamin Franklin. Van Doren was also the author of *Swift* (1930), and *The Roving Critic* (1950), among other books. In the following extract, he comments on the social formalism of *The Age of Innocence*.]

At the outset of the twentieth century O. Henry, in a mood of reaction from current snobbism, discovered what he called the Four Million; and during the same years, in a mood not wholly different, Edith Wharton rediscovered what she would never have called the Four Hundred. Or rather she made known to the considerable public which peeps at fashionable New York through the obliging windows of fiction that that world was not so simple in its magnificence as the inquisitive, but uninstructed, had been led to believe. Behind the splendors reputed to characterize the great, she testified on almost every page of her books, lay certain arcana which if much duller were also much more desirable. Those splendors were merely as noisy brass to the finer metal of the authentic inner circles. These were very small, and they suggested an American aristocracy rather less than they suggested the aborigines of their native continent.

Ralph Marvell in *The Custom of the Country* described Washington Square as the "Reservation," and prophesied that "before long its inhabitants would be exhibited at ethnological shows, pathetically engaged in the exercise of their primitive industries." Mrs. Wharton has exhibited them in the exercise of industries not precisely primitive, and yet aboriginal enough, very largely concerned in turning shapely shoulders to the hosts of Americans anxious and determined to invade their ancient reservations. As the success of the women in keeping new aspirants out of drawing-room and country house has always been greater than the success of the men in keeping them out of Wall Street, the aboriginal aristocracy in Mrs. Wharton's novels transacts its affairs for the most part in drawing-rooms and country houses. There, however, to judge by *The House of Mirth*, *The Custom of the Country*, and *The Age of Innocence*, the life of the inhabitants, far from being a continuous revel as represented by the popular novelists, is marked by nothing so much as an uncompromising decorum.

⟨. . .⟩ Newland Archer and Ellen Olenska in *The Age of Innocence* neither lose nor seek an established position within the social mandarinate of Manhattan as constituted in the seventies of the last century. They belong there and there they remain. But at what sacrifices of personal happiness and spontaneous action! They walk through their little drama with the unadventurous stride of puppets; they observe dozens of taboos with a respect allied to terror. It is true that they appear to have been the victims of the provincial "innocence" of their generation, but the newer generation in New York is not entirely acquitted of a certain complicity in the formalism of its past.

From the first Mrs. Wharton's power has lain in the ability to reproduce in fiction the circumstances of a compact community in a way that illustrates the various oppressions which such communities put upon individual vagaries, whether viewed as sin, or ignorance, or folly, or merely as social impossibility.

—Carl Van Doren, *Contemporary American Novelists* 1900–1920 (New York: Macmillan, 1922), pp. 95–96, 97

Q. D. LEAVIS ON EDITH WHARTON'S ANALYT-ICAL STYLE

[Q. D. Leavis (1906–1981) was an influential author, lec-
turer, and critic. She wrote *Fiction and the Reading Public*
(1932) and edited the journal *Scrutiny* with her husband,
the celebrated critic F. R. Leavis. In the following extract,
originally published in *Scrutiny,* Leavis comments on
Edith Wharton's analysis, rather than observance, of the
society she describes in her historical fiction.]

I think it eventually becomes a question of what the novelist has
to offer us, either directly or by implication, in the way of positives. In *The Bunner Sisters, Summer,* and some other places, Mrs.
Wharton rests upon the simple goodness of the decent poor, as
indeed George Eliot and Wordsworth both do in part—that is,
the most widespread common factor of moral worth. But
beyond that Mrs. Wharton has only negatives, her values
emerging I suppose as something other than what she exposes
as worthless. This is not very nourishing, and it is on similar
grounds that Flaubert, so long admired as the ideal artist of the
novel, has begun to lose esteem. It seems to be the fault of the
disintegrating and spiritually impoverished society she analyzes.
Her value is that she does analyze and is not content to reflect.
We may contrast Jane Austen, who does not even analyze, but,
having the good fortune to have been born into a flourishing culture, can take for granted its foundations and accept its standards, working within them on a basis of internal relations
entirely. The common code of her society is a valuable one and
she benefits from it as an artist. Mr. Knightley's speech to
Emma, reproving her for snubbing Miss Bates, is a useful
instance: manners there are seen to be based on moral values.
Mrs. Wharton's worthy people are all primitives or archaic survivals. This inability to find any significance in the society that
she spent her prime in, or to find "significance only through
what its frivolity destroys," explains the absence of poetry in her
disposition and of many kinds of valuable experience in her
books. She has none of that natural piety, that richness of feeling
and sense of a moral order, of experience as a process of
growth, in which George Eliot's local criticisms are embedded

and which give the latter her large stature. Between her conviction that the new society she grew up into was vicious and insecurely based on an ill-used working class and her conviction that her inherited mode of living represented a dead end, she could find no foundation to build on. We may see where her real strength lay in the critical phrases she uses: "Her moral muscles had become atrophied [by buying] off suffering with money, or denying its existence with words]"; "the superficial contradictions and accommodations of a conscience grown elastic from too much use"—and in the short story "Autres Temps . . ." a study of the change in moral codes she had witnessed since her youth. Here the divorced mother, who had for many years hidden her disgrace in Florence, returns to America to succor, as she thinks, her divorced and newly remarried daughter. At first, finding the absence of any prejudice against divorce in the new America, she is exalted, then she feels in her bewilderment "'I didn't take up much room before, but now where is there a corner for me?' . . . Where indeed in this crowded, topsy-turvy world, with its headlong changes and helter-skelter readjustments, its new tolerances and indifferences and accommodations, was there room for a character fashioned by slower sterner processes and a life broken under their inexorable pressure?" And finally, depressed by what she feels to be the lack of any kind of moral taste, she loses her illusions about the real benefits of such a change, she finds it to be merely a change in social fashions and not a revolution bringing genuine enlightenment based on good feeling. She explains to an old friend: "'Traditions that have lost their meaning are the hardest of all to destroy . . . We're shut up in a little tight round of habit and association, just as we're shut up in this room. . . . We're all imprisoned, of course—all of us middling people, who don't carry freedom in our brains. But we've accommodated ourselves to our different cells, and if we're moved suddenly into new ones we're likely to find a stone wall where we thought there was air, and to knock ourselves senseless against it.'" She chooses to return to Florence, "moving again among the grim edges of reality."

—Q. D. Leavis, "Henry James's Heiress: The Importance of Edith Wharton (1938)," *Edith Wharton: A Collection of Critical Essays*, ed. Irving Howe (Englewood Cliffs, NJ: Prentice-Hall, 1962), pp. 86–88

❖

EDMUND WILSON ON EDITH WHARTON'S CENTRAL MALE CHARACTERS

[Edmund Wilson (1895–1972) was one of the most influential critics of the 20th century. He was editor and contributor at various times for *Vanity Fair, New Republic*, and *The New Yorker*. He is the author of the classic *Axel's Castles: A Study in the Imaginative Literature of 1870–1930* (1931) and *Patriotic Gore: Studies in the Literature of the American Civil War* (1962). In this extract, Wilson discusses Wharton's treatment of Newland Archer as one of her "timid American male" characters.]

If we compare *The Age of Innocence* with Henry James's *Europeans,* whose central situation it reproduces, the pupil's divergence from the master is seen in the most striking way. In both cases, a Europeanized American woman—Baroness Münster, Countess Olenska—returns to the United States to intrude upon and disturb the existence of a conservative provincial society; in both cases, she attracts and almost captivates an intelligent man of the community who turns out, in the long run, to be unable to muster the courage to take her, and who allows her to go back to Europe. Henry James makes of this a balanced comedy of the conflict between the Bostonian and the cosmopolitan points of view (so he reproached her with not having developed the theme of Undine Spragg's marriage with a French nobleman in terms of French and American manners, as he had done with a similar one in *The Reverberator*); but in Edith Wharton's version one still feels an active resentment against the pusillanimity of the provincial group and also, as in other of her books, a special complaint against the timid American male who has let the lady down.

Up through *The Age of Innocence,* and recurring at all points of her range from *The House of Mirth* to *Ethan Frome*, the typical masculine figure in Edith Wharton's fiction is a man set apart from his neighbors by education, intellect and feeling, but lacking the force or the courage either to impose himself or to get away. She generalizes about this type in the form in which she knew it best in her autobiographical volume: 'They combined a cultivated taste with marked social gifts,' she says; but 'their weakness was that, save in a few cases, they made so little use of their ability'": they were content to 'live in dilettantish leisure,' rendering none of 'the public services that a more enlightened social system would have exacted of them.' But she had described a very common phenomenon of the America of after the Civil War. Lawrence Selden, the city lawyer, who sits comfortably in his bachelor apartment with his flowerbox of mignonette and his first edition of La Bruyère and allows Lily Bart to drown, is the same person as Lawyer Royall of *Summer*, with his lofty orations and his drunken lapses. One could have found him during the big-business era in almost any American city or town: the man of superior abilities who had the impulse toward self-improvement and independence, but who had been more or less rendered helpless by the surf of headlong money-making and spending which carried him along with its breakers or left him stranded on the New England hills—in either case thwarted and stunted by the mediocre level of the community. In Edith Wharton's novels these men are usually captured and dominated by women of conventional morals and middle-class ideals; when an exceptional woman comes along who is thirsting for something different and better, the man is unable to give it to her. This special situation Mrs. Wharton, with some conscious historical criticism but chiefly impelled by a feminine animus, has dramatized with much vividness and intelligence. There are no first-rate men in these novels.

—Edmund Wilson, *The Wound and the Bow: Seven Studies in Literature* (New York: Oxford University Press, 1947), pp. 206–08

BLAKE NEVIUS ON WHARTON'S USE OF IRONY IN *THE AGE OF INNOCENCE*

[Blake Nevius (b. 1916), a noted literary critic, is a professor of English at the University of California at Los

Angeles. He is the author of critical works on Robert Herrick, Sinclair Lewis, and Edith Wharton, from which the following extract was taken.]

The Age of Innocence is not Mrs. Wharton's strongest novel, but, along with *Ethan Frome,* it is the one in which she is most thoroughly the artist. It is a triumph of style, of the perfect adaptation of means to a conception fully grasped from the outset. It would be difficult to say that she faltered or overreached at any point. The movement of her plot may be established by the successive and clearly marked positions taken by Newland Archer in his relations with Ellen Olenska and May Welland. May Welland personifies all the evasions and compromises of his clan; she is the "safe" alternative; whereas Ellen has the "mysterious faculty of suggesting tragic and moving possibilities outside the daily run of experience." Charmed by May's innocence, and about to announce his engagement to her, Archer at first finds it easy to join old New York in condemning the Mingotts for sponsoring Countess Olenska: "Few things seemed to Newland Archer more awful than an offence against 'Taste,' that far-off divinity of whom 'Form' was the mere visible representative and vice-regent." He is the willing accomplice of a society "wholly absorbed in barricading itself against the unpleasant," and his appreciation of May Welland is based on this precarious ideal: "Nothing about his betrothed pleased him more than her resolute determination to carry to its utmost limits that ritual of ignoring the 'unpleasant' in which they had both been brought up." In the story that follows Edith Wharton tries to make clear what this innocence costs. The measure of change wrought in Archer's outlook by his experience with Ellen is suggested by a sentence occurring midway in the novel, before the echo of his earlier belief has quite died away: "Ah, no, he did not want May to have that kind of innocence, the innocence that seals the mind against imagination and the heart against experience!"

His fall from grace is carefully motivated. Old New York's treatment of Countess Olenska eventually arouses the innate sense of chivalry that he shares with Ralph Marvell, and once he has read the divorce evidence his indifference is vanquished: "she stood before him as an exposed and pitiful figure, to be saved at all costs from farther wounding herself in her mad plunges against fate." In spite of his strict notions, he is not entirely unprepared for a sentimental adventure. One of the first things we learn about him is that he has had an affair with a married woman "whose charms had held his fancy through two mildly agitated years." Once he has accepted Ellen's case—ironically at the instigation of the clan—he is compelled by logic and sympathy, and finally by the deeper reasons of love, to adopt her point of view. Nothing in Edith Wharton's treatment of the situation is more subtly expressed than the changes which Archer's affair with Ellen work in his perceptions. But his freedom is won too late. Ellen has at the same time learned something from him. She has accepted seriously one of the lessons he had mastered by rote and passed on to her: that freedom cannot be purchased at another's cost. It makes no difference that he is now prepared to discard it. He has given her an idea by which to live and, in doing so, destroyed the one means of enlarging his new-found freedom. When he returns to May Welland, it is to the ultimate realization that, like John Marcher in James's "The Beast in the Jungle," he is the man "to whom nothing was ever to happen."

Edith Wharton never surpassed the irony in which she enveloped this play of cross-purposes. "It is impossible to be ironical," she once noted, "without having a sense of the infinitudes." To the novelist so equipped, the complacent worldliness of old New York offered fair game. Irony was the method best suited to her temperament and her material. It was her way of telling the world that she had not been taken in, whatever her allegiances: and it was the only alternative to tragedy, which, as she suggested in novel after novel, was impossible in her world. It was an atmosphere, however, in which a reader such as Katherine Mansfield, for all her admiration of *The Age of Innocence,* found it increasingly difficult to breathe, for Mrs. Wharton's self-control got on her nerves until she asked, quite irrelevantly in this instance at least, whether it was vulgar "to entreat a little wildness, a dark place or two in the soul."

—Blake Nevius, *Edith Wharton: A Study of Her Fiction* (Berkeley: University of California Press, 1953), pp. 185–87

VIOLA HOPKINS ON IMAGERY IN *THE AGE OF INNOCENCE*

[Viola Hopkins (b. 1928) is an author, critic, and research associate at the University of Virginia. Her critical works include *Henry James and the Visual Arts* (1970), and she is the editor of *Henry James: Modern Judgements* (1968). In this extract, Hopkins explores Wharton's use of rich descriptive detail in *The Age of Innocence*.]

[Wharton's] rationale for creating detailed background was that "the bounds of a personality are not reproducible by a sharp black line, but . . . each of us flows imperceptibly into adjacent people and things." And certainly her use of detail never degenerates into mere reporting or local color. Their library characterizes the Archers; Ellen's *décolletage* as well as the reactions to it at the opera "places" for us dramatically both Ellen and New York society and reveals important shades of differences in taste and custom that presage further conflict and complications. Like the fabrics and household objects in Dutch paintings, the interiors and details of dress of Mrs. Wharton's New Yorkers are richly suggestive of the inner life of their owners.

The descriptive detail, moreover, constitutes in itself a kind of imagery; for example, May's wedding dress is first of all a costume of blue-white satin and old lace. The fact that, like the other women of her set, she wears her wedding dress for the first year or two of marriage is a concrete detail adding to our picture of this frugal, essentially bourgeois upper class. Finally, May's torn and mudstained wedding dress becomes symbolic of the stains on her marriage made by Archer's passion for Ellen.

The actual verbal imagery also reflects the New York world and mode of speech. Mrs. Wharton's writing is not studded with striking, extended, or violent metaphors. Sometimes her writing even suffers from excessive reliance on faded or tired metaphors and similes such as are not uncommon in conversation: a word falls "like a bombshell"; bandages are taken off eyes; Newland did not have a "blank page to offer his bride in exchange for the unblemished one she was to give him"; if he had been as sheltered as she had been "they would have been no more fit to find their way about than the Babes in the Wood"; Catherine "slept like a baby"; Ellen's words "fell into his breast like burning lead". More neatly finished but no less conventional is the comparison of marriage to a haven: "Marriage was not the safe anchorage he had been taught to think, but a voyage on uncharted seas." As one would expect of a traditionally educated person, the well-known classical myths are alluded to casually. Jane "hovered Cassandra-like"; Ellen's actions followed her emotions with "Olympian speed"; May is frequently referred to as "Diana-like." More specific literary allusions usually have a source in Newland's reading or in plays he has seen. For example, he makes the connection between van der Luyden's determined protection of Ellen and the zeal of the main character in *Le Voyage de M. Perrichon* in clinging to the young man he had rescued.

While some of the imagery is so neutral as to be unnoticeable, several types of recurring images mostly governed by Newland's point of view call into question the values of the world which he had heretofore taken for granted. The "anthropological" image, for example, drawn from recent books Newland has been reading, appears on the second page and permeates the novel. "What was or was not 'the thing' played a part as important in Newland Archer's New York as the inscrutable totem terrors that had ruled the destinies of his forefathers thousands of years ago." New York families are constantly referred to as "tribes" or "clans." The New York wedding was "a rite that seemed to belong to the dawn of history." "Concealment of the spot in which the bridal night was to be spent [was] one of the most sacred taboos of the prehistoric ritual." "He saw in a flash that if the family had ceased to consult him it was because some deep tribal instinct warned them that he was no longer on their side." May's dinner for Ellen was "the tribal rally around a kinswoman about to be eliminated from the tribe." This pervasive "tribal" imagery is one means by which Newland's little world is seen in perspective, its ethnocentrism exposed, and its "civilization" shown to be unflatteringly primitive.

—Viola Hopkins, "The Ordering Style of *The Age of Innocence*," *American Literature* 30, No. 3 (November 1958): 353–54

❖

LOUIS AUCHINCLOSS ON THE REMINISCENT NATURE OF *THE AGE OF INNOCENCE*

[Louis Auchincloss (b. 1923), a novelist, short-story writer, and literary critic, has written a number of critical works, including *On Sister Carrie* (1968), *Reading Henry James* (1975), and *False Dawn: Women in the Age of the Sun King* (1985). In the following extract, Auchincloss discusses the setting of Wharton's novel and its similarities to the New York of her childhood.]

The title, *The Age of Innocence,* refers to the New York of the 1870's in the girlhood of Edith Jones and gives to the book the flavor of a historical novel, as is often pointed out by critics. The fact not always recognized by critics is that it was a habit of Victorian novelists to set their stories in the era of their childhood. The novelist of manners has since shown a tendency to revert to a usually recent past where social distinctions, which make up so much of his subject matter, were more sharply defined, or at least where he thinks they were. *The Age of Innocence* (1920) is written in a Proustian mood of remembered things that evokes the airless atmosphere of an old, ordered, small-town New York as vividly as a conversation piece by Eastman Johnson. Here the dilettante bachelor, Newland Archer, as usual a lawyer, is at last placed in a story adapted to bring out the best and the worst in him. For he must have enough passion and imagination to aspire to break through the barriers of convention that surround him and yet be weak enough so that he cannot finally escape the steely embrace of an aroused tribe. Newland knows that he never really has a chance from the beginning; that is his pathos. He is engaged to May Welland, and he will marry May Welland and spend a lifetime with May Welland, and that is that, and both he and May's beautiful, Europeanized, disenchanted cousin, Ellen Olenska, realize it and accept it.

We have a suffocating sense of a creature trapped and doomed as poor Newland comes to the awareness, from the exchanged glances, coughs, and silences that surround him, that all of his vast family and family-in-law, including his own wife, are convinced that he is enjoying the very affair that he has failed to achieve and are united in irresistible tact to cut it short. But Mrs. Wharton is not suggesting that Newland and Ellen, in their renunciation of each other, have condemned themselves to a life of unrewarding frustration. Rules and regulations have now their validity to her, no matter what passions they crush. "It was you," Ellen tells Archer, "who made me understand that under the dullness there are things so fine and sensitive and delicate that even those I most cared for in my other life look cheap in comparison." And a generation later Archer sees no cause to repine in thinking back over his married life with May: "Their long years together had shown him that it did not so much matter if marriage was a dull duty, as long as it kept the dignity of a duty: lapsing from that, it became a mere battle of ugly appetites. Looking about him, he honored his own past, and mourned for it. After all, there was good in the old ways."

It is Edith Wharton's tribute to her own background, this affirmation that under the thick, smoky glass of convention bloom the fine, fragile flowers of patient suffering and self-sacrifice. To run away from society may be as vulgar in the end as to crash it. Newland Archer builds a shrine in his heart around the image of Ellen from which he derives strength to endure his uneventful and moderately useful life, a life where civic and social duties are judiciously balanced and where the impetus of Theodore Roosevelt even gets him into the state legislature, if only for a single term. We see him more completely than any other of Mrs. Wharton's heroes, and the reader who doubts that such a type existed has only to turn the pages of the voluminous diary of George Templeton Strong, published long after Edith Wharton's death.

—Louis Auchincloss, *Edith Wharton* (Minneapolis, MN: University of Minnesota Press, 1961), pp. 29–30

GRACE KELLOGG SHAW SMITH ON THE CHARACTERS AND MERITS OF *THE AGE OF INNOCENCE*

[Grace Kellogg Shaw Smith, an author and literary critic, wrote *The Two Lives of Edith Wharton: The Woman and Her Work* (1965), from which this extract was taken. Smith notes that, although *The Age of Innocence* is appreciated primarily as a comedy of manners, it is actually a much deeper, more intimate story.]

The triumph of *The Age of Innocence* has been confirmed in the more than four decades since its publication. Mrs. Wharton portrayed the society of her young womanhood with a clarity and a firmness of outline that have given them life and permanent importance. *The Age of Innocence* is a flawless piece of artistry. The lambent fires that play beneath never flare up to disrupt the cool and decorous surface. A delicate veil of nostalgia hangs, hardly palpable, between the author and her remembered scene. Love it she must, though no sentimental compassion makes her keen, swift stroke falter. The irony is delicate—nothing heavy-handed about it. It does not destroy at any point the web of poignant beauty.

The novel immortalized a period and a class in American society which had vanished and of which modern America would have lost all knowledge but for its chronicler. It is by this unique value as a social record that the importance of *The Age of Innocence* is ordinarily gauged. Nevius has said, "It was precisely [the] pictorial quality [of its period and scene] that attracted Edith Wharton and enabled her to demonstrate once again that she had the 'visualizing power' beyond any other novelist of her time." But to call *The Age of Innocence* a comedy of manners does not quite describe it: it has far more an elegiac quality.

This is a story in which the reader's sensibilities deeply engage with the fortunes of the persons of the drama. Newland Archer lives in the pages. So does the lovely Ellen Olenska—lovely not only in the flesh, but in her quick spirit, in the generous impulses of her heart and in the strength of her characters. This effect of full creation is not limited to Newland and Ellen. May Welland, the Archer women, the van der Luydens, Mrs. Manson

Mingott—all of them live and move and have their being fully and completely. The vitality of the persons of the cast, the poignancy of the drama played out entirely below the surface—what Nevius calls the "impeccable, sophisticated surface"—forbid any such easy classification of this novel as has sometimes been made.

Not one of Edith Wharton's characteristic faults flaws the book. No importunate epigrams divert attention from the vein of silver light: not a single unwarranted coincidence mars the sequence of cause and effect; no character is scanted in the drawing, no scene is tossed off in a hurry.

Perfection, it is true, may be an adverse element, destroying by its exactions something more vital and powerful. Not here. To say of *The Age of Innocence* that it has perfection is only a way of saying that not a single imperfection detracts from the whole. The hand of the author never falters. From the first word to the last, every thread is firmly held. Before pen is set to paper she has the whole plot in her palm. The end is known to her from the beginning. Her book has economy of style, economy of incident, economy of emotion. The story moves inexorably from the moment when Archer looks across the opera house and sees the disgraced Ellen Olenska in the box occupied by his betrothed and her mother to the moment when as the lights go on, a quarter of a century later, in Ellen's Paris flat, he rises from a park bench and turns stiffly away. Not once is the quiet tragedy coerced.

The denouement is inevitable. That Newland, at this last moment should retreat from putting his fate to the touch, has been presaged by his retreat from every crisis of the tale that has preceded it. Edith Wharton has been charged, and perhaps all too justly, with "loading the dice" against an unhappy heroine or a pair of unfortunate lovers. She has been charged with denying the happy ending to more than one story that could have had it. The charge cannot be brought against *The Age of Innocence*. The end was in its beginning and in every step of its progress.

—Grace Kellogg Shaw Smith, *The Two Lives of Edith Wharton: The Woman and Her Work* (New York: Appleton-Century, 1965), pp. 227–28

❖

ARTHUR MIZENER ON SOME FLAWS IN *THE AGE OF INNOCENCE*

[Arthur Mizener (1907–1988) was the chairman of the English Department at Cornell University and a noted critic of the modern novel. He is the author of *The Far Side of Paradise: A Biography of F. Scott Fitzgerald* (1951) and *The Saddest Story: A Biography of Ford Madox Ford* (1971). In the following extract from his book *Twelve Great American Novels,* Mizener remarks on some flaws of character delineation in Wharton's novel.]

The Age of Innocence is very nearly a great novel, though it would be no service to it to pretend that it is some kind of miracle wholly without evidence of the limitations so prominent in Mrs. Wharton's other work. Her impulse to illustrate her views instead of to represent meaningful experience occasionally appears in it, though never in a way to damage it seriously. It is only an annoyance when she cannot resist the temptation to let a series of accidents send Newland Archer and May Welland to spend their honeymoon in the patroon's house on the van der Luyden's estate, where Newland had first recognized, too late, that he loved Ellen Olenska; or that at the crisis of Newland's frustration by his stiflingly conventional marriage, she should have him throw open the library window (on "reality" of course) and announce portentously that "I shall never be happy unless I can open windows." The worst of these displays of cleverness is perhaps the way she has May tear her wedding dress when Newland is longing to run off with Ellen. May's wearing her wedding dress to the opera that night because she believes she is pregnant is at once a fine expression of her character and a gesture that focuses a good many of the novel's conflicting attitudes. But her tearing its hem as she and Newland arrive home is, even as an accident, wholly unlike her, and Mrs. Wharton forces this accident onto the action in order to create a crude and even sentimental symbol for the novel's feelings about Newland's marriage.

Once or twice, too, she forces her material irresponsibly to make mere social comments, as when she presses the contrast between Fanny Beaufort, the illegitimate daughter of the novel's unscrupulous financier whom Newland Archer's son marries, and Ellen Olenska, whom Newland loved but renounced. In order to stress this contrast between the customs of the two ages, she describes the world Fanny Beaufort lives in as more untrammeled by any customs than it is easy to believe possible or than Edith Wharton, of all people, could ever have seriously believed, and makes the later life of Fanny's father one of a responsible domesticity wholly inconsistent with the splendidly gross and unscrupulous man he has been throughout the novel.

But these limiting displays of cleverness are insignificant in the book and never affect the main action. Throughout that action her intelligence, with its cultivated powers of analysis and construction, is used to give dramatic emphasis to the experience of characters and ways of life that are alive in her imagination. The difference that makes is evident in the success she has with the love affair of Newland Archer and Ellen Olenska, whose passion and whose refusal to be self-deceived she makes beautifully vivid and convincing. Having made us see the insights and ignorances both of them have acquired from the ways they have lived, she also makes their love for one another almost inevitable, and the frustration of that love inescapable. It would be hard to overpraise the dramatic skill and economy with which she brings these things about. The novel's opening sequence of scenes illustrates them clearly. In addition to establishing the senses of life that govern Newland Archer and Ellen Olenska, these scenes must create for us the context in which their love has its existence, the little world in which old New York, with its incurious ignorance of great reaches of reality, is conducting its stubborn, doomed battle to resist the encroachments of the powerful, unscrupulous, and often brutal *nouveaux riches*, whose ambition it is to be a part of old New York society.

—Arthur Mizener, *Twelve Great American Novels* (New York: The New American Library, 1967), pp. 78–80

❧

R. W. B. Lewis on The Societal Obstacles between Newland Archer and Countess Olenska

[R. W. B. Lewis (b. 1917) is a Senior Fellow of the School of Letters at Indiana University. He is the author of several literary works, including *The American Adam: Innocence, Tragedy, and Tradition in the Nineteenth Century* (1955) and *Edith Wharton: A Biography*, for which he was awarded a Pulitzer Prize in 1976. In the following extract, Lewis comments on Wharton's treatment of the relationship between Newland Archer and Countess Olenska.]

With the excuse of visiting a stud-farm, Newland rides to Portsmouth, only to learn to his bleak dismay that Mme. Olenska has been called to Boston. He makes his way to Boston and has enquiries made at the Parker House; Countess Olenska has gone out. He encounters her by chance seated under a tree in the Boston Common; but their conversation remains strained amid the crowd that comes and goes along the path. They drive to the wharf and board a paddle-steamer that carries passengers on tours around the bay. Here they come closer, in a communion of "blessed silence"; but when they enter the dining-room, they find it packed with "a strident party of innocent-looking men and women" (surrogates for the innocent-seeming New Yorkers Newland had fled in the summer resort). He asks for a private room; and there, at last, they communicate their love—in half-spoken words, in a touch of hands.

What is especially moving, as well as technically superb, in that closing scene is that even in that so hard-earned privacy, their communication can only be partial. Or rather and more subtly: their reticent declaration of love must contain within it a shared awareness of the profound moral obstacles that still divide them. Any expression of love between the husband of May Welland and the wife of Count Olenski must include an acknowledgement of their moral situation; though for all that, there must be no further holding back from full expression. All of this is conveyed at a stroke by Mme. Olenska's physical gesture—"Her outstretched hands . . ." fell into his, while her arms, extended but not rigid, kept him far enough off to let her surrendered face say the rest."

It is the sensitive and expert dramatization of place throughout the novel—as a way of making visible and palpable the conflict between the social and the personal, and the moral issues involved—that lends a kind of finality of meaning to Countess Olenska's response some chapters later. I have always found this passage as poignant and as unsentimental as anything Edith Wharton ever wrote. Archer is escorting Mme. Olenska back from the Pennsylvania terminus, and something moves him to insist that they will, somehow, have a life together. Mme. Olenska asks with sudden harshness whether it is Archer's idea that she should live with him as his mistress. Poor Archer says, stammering: "I want somehow to get away with you into a world where words like that—categories like that—won't exist"; and to this Mme. Olenska replies with a sigh and a laugh: "Oh, my dear—where is that country? Have you ever been there?"

—R. W. B. Lewis, Introduction to The Age of Innocence (New York: Scribner's, 1968), pp. xii–xiii

GARY H. LINDBERG ON EDITH WHARTON'S NARRATIVE STRATEGY IN *THE AGE OF INNOCENCE*

[Gary H. Lindberg (b. 1941) is a literary critic and an associate professor of English at the University of New Hampshire. He is the author of *Edith Wharton and the Novel of Manners* (1975) and *The Confidence Man in American Literature* (1982). Here, Lindberg outlines Wharton's narrative strategy in *The Age of Innocence*.]

In *The Age of Innocence* the ⟨. . .⟩ narrative strategy encloses the central moral decision of the novel, for in the transition between books 1 and 2 Archer chooses between Ellen Olenska and May Welland. Having declared his love to Ellen at the end of book 1, Archer asserts that his new self-awareness makes marriage to May unthinkable, whereas Ellen argues from Archer's own earlier pronouncements about duty to the community and in particular to May. It is not certain that Ellen will be able to maintain her sincere reasoning, nor is it clear that Archer can even understand her argument. The arrival of May's telegram, announcing an early wedding, breaks up the deliberation. Book 2 opens at the wedding. Here, instead of accounting for lapsed time by postulating a chain of consequences, the reader is forced into Archer's bewildered sense of what has happened. The very rapidity of the sequence leaves no time to consider whether May's telegram should have changed everything again for Archer; the sudden movement shows what power a simple public gesture, here a telegram, can have when backed by a network of social obligations and inward habits. Furthermore, the interval between the telegram and the wedding virtually vanishes, as if the latter were the immediate and the only recognizable consequence of the former. Momentarily, then, Wharton's arrangement of interstices engages the reader in Archer's own illusion that May's announcement eliminates moral choice entirely.

In its immediate implications this narrative strategy does not suggest an external doom hanging over the characters; rather it increases the moral seriousness of their conduct. The sequences begin in private moral dilemmas, and the hypothesized determinations and effects with which the reader fills in the narrative gaps simply measure the personal results of the implied decisions. But the choices made in each case can easily be construed as non-choices; to the character, the matter seems out of his hands, and even to author and reader the moral agent is not deliberating but following the course of least immediate difficulty. It is the power of social expectancies, reinforced by the pressure of public time, that creates for the character the illusion that only one line of action is even imaginable. Thus, insofar as Wharton's handling of narrative gaps makes us comply in projecting and understanding deterministic sequences, we tacitly acknowledge what personal strength and clarity of insight would be necessary before a character could even contemplate a course of action other than that determined by public pressure. The effect of these narrative gaps is often emphasized, as in the treatment of Archer's wedding, by their coinciding with a sudden passage from a private to a public scene, as if the character's implicit failure to accept his own accountability reduced him to a mere fragment of the communal world.

—Gary H. Lindberg, *Edith Wharton and the Novel of Manners* (Charlottesville, VA: University Press of Virginia, 1975), pp. 48–49

Margaret B. McDowall on Newland Archer's Limited Views

[Margaret B. McDowall (b. 1923) is chairperson of women's studies and an associate professor at the University of Iowa. In this extract from her 1976 work on Wharton, McDowall discusses Newland Archer's conventionality.]

In the opening scene Newland Archer finds the "innocence" of May Welland, his betrothed, appealing. When he attends the opera with her, he assumes with approval that she cannot even recognize Faust's intent to seduce Margaret. But gradually he resents the probability that she will shut herself away from life, as her mother has, by refusing to become involved in the problems of others. Placid Mrs. Welland, in her "invincible innocence," excuses herself from listening to Ellen Olenska's troubles because she must keep her mind "bright and happy" for the sake of her slightly ailing husband. Even before Newland's marriage, he realizes with a shock that he does not want May to be like her mother. He wants more than Mrs. Welland's "innocence that seals the mind against imagination and the heart against experience."

Although Archer does not evince Mrs. Welland's naïveté, he never fully recognizes his own conventionality. Considering himself capable of teaching May the value of music and books, he nevertheless has little interest in learning about the great world outside his own circle; and he finds comfort in the stability of New York society. Though he believes that cultural interests such as the opera have enlarged his mind, he is so limited by exclusive traditions that he expresses relief that the opera house is too small to accommodate the newly rich. He accepts the idea that all German texts of French operas sung by Swedish performers should be translated into Italian for American audiences—just as he accepts "all the other conventions on which his life was moulded." All aspects of Archer's life fall into settled patterns, and his indecisiveness prevents him from rebelling against those forces that constrict the spontaneous expression of the self and that encourage him to overlook evils demanding rectification. His conventionality is symbolized by the routine parting of his hair with two silver-backed brushes, the flower in his lapel, and his provincial pride at being a New Yorker, though he regards himself, ironically, as cosmopolitan.

Edith Wharton revealed Archer's limited views, subtly and ironically, at the very times that he is evaluating complacently, from the heights of his presumed sophistication, the limited views of others, particularly those of May and Ellen. Charmed by Ellen Olenska's imagination and experience, he nevertheless reacts with hypocritical conservatism when he refuses to acknowledge her need to divorce a cruel, unfaithful husband. To recognize openly her bitter experience would be to acknowledge that a woman of his wife's family knows too much about sex. Archer's temptation to be unfaithful to May ultimately helps him achieve a greater honesty about himself; he is now able to recognize that passion and moral convention can sometimes be strongly at odds with each other. As a result of his admitting his own passions and his ultimate desire for an illicit affair with Ellen, he attains a degree of tolerance for those outside his own circle of complacent and morally "superior" aristocrats.

Regarding his relatives and friends as the whole world early in the book, he assumes that Ellen's naïveté prevents her from being impressed by the party that the van der Luydens give for her. In Archer's circle, everyone recognizes that this party is the van der Luydens' gesture of acceptance of Ellen—an acceptance reluctantly accorded by other aristocrats since she has returned to New York without her husband. As a matter of fact, Ellen's worldly knowledge makes her refuse to attach to the party the radical significance that Archer and his friends see in it. Ellen wants only to be accepted for what she is, not forgiven for something that is not her fault. Because Newland's friends still believe in the import of such social gestures, the farewell party that May gives for Ellen also assumes importance because it symbolizes for them the end of Newland's presumed affair with Ellen.

If he initially misjudges Ellen for her failure to react according to his expectations at the time of the van der Luydens' party, he also misjudges May by viewing her as more limited than she is. Before their marriage, he simply assumes that she will never be capable of surprising him with "a new idea, a weakness, a cruelty, or an emotion." He is himself incapable at this time of recognizing her resentment of his affair with Mrs. Rushworth or her courage at suggesting that he marry his former mistress. He does not recognize the stratagems to which May resorts in order to keep him from leaving with Ellen, nor does he realize her lasting gratitude to him for giving up Ellen. His egocentric temperament, which limits his imagination, prevents him from seeing May as a woman instead of a stereotype. He never sees that what he calls "her abysmal purity" is a myth largely of his own formulation—one that underestimates her intelligence and the extent of her worldly knowledge.

—Margaret B. McDowell, *Edith Wharton* (Boston: Twayne Publishers, 1976), pp. 97–98

CYNTHIA GRIFFIN WOLFF ON *THE AGE OF INNOCENCE* AND HENRY JAMES'S *PORTRAIT OF A LADY*

[Cynthia Griffin Wolff (b. 1936) is an associate professor of English at the University of Massachusetts at

Amherst. She has authored *Samuel Richardson and the Eighteenth-Century Puritan Character* (1972) and *A Feast of Words: The Triumph of Edith Wharton* (1977), from which this extract was taken.]

The Age of Innocence had many meanings for Edith Wharton. It borrows more extensively from the ambiance of her childhood world than any other novel she published; and it is explicitly called to the reader's attention that Newland Archer is fifty-seven at the conclusion of the novel, Wharton's own age in 1919 when she began writing it. Yet perhaps the central meaning grows out of the complex way in which the novel beckons to Wharton's dearest friend, Henry James.

The communication begins, most fittingly, with a complicated joke: *The Age of Innocence* is the title of a well-known portrait by Reynolds which hangs in the National Gallery; it is the portrait of a lady—a very young lady, to be sure, a little girl in fact. Nevertheless, the reference converts Wharton's title into a private pun. James's novel *The Portrait of a Lady* was Wharton's favorite among his many books (the only one ever to appear on her list of "favorite books"). In the name of her own novel, Wharton announces the antiphonal relationship between her work and James's in the way that *he* would have understood best. There is no mistaking her intention, for at the same time that she converted the working title of "Old New York" into "The Age of Innocence," she also changed the name of her hero to "Newland" Archer, an American who elects to remain at home in the New World only to have Old World temptations and knowledge come to him. That Newland Archer is intended as a parallel to Isabel Archer is further emphasized by Ned Winsett's remark to him: "You're like the pictures on the walls of a deserted house: 'The Portrait of a Gentleman.'"

These resemblances are merely verbal plays, casual allusions meant to convey deeper connections between Wharton's work and James's. Wharton intended neither parody nor one-to-one borrowing: Newland is not Isabel's exact counterpart—nor is Ellen, though Ellen's marriage and her tragic knowledge certainly do recall Isabel's. Rather, Wharton used these allusions to James much as eighteenth-century satirists used references to classical epics as a way of conveying a sense of moral seriousness and a similarity of concern. If "The Age of Innocence" describes the stable pre-World War I society of old New York to which Wharton was making a private pilgrimage, it also describes a prelapsarian state. Thus while James explores the notion of a "fortunate fall" in *The Portrait of a Lady,* in *The Age of Innocence* Wharton examines the value of choosing not to be corrupted. Moreover, Wharton and James focus their intense moral scrutiny on similar concerns, particularly the problem of the right to individual "freedom" as measured against the binding sanctity of the commitment to the institution of marriage.

In the end, however, Wharton's novel is a balancing companion piece to James's; for while James is interested in exploring the world an American Puritan might discover by moving away from New World prejudices, Wharton's thrust is in the opposite direction, back into the shaping culture in which her American hero was born. Implicit in the imperative to come back "for good" is a notion of maturity very similar to the one that Erik Erikson has articulated for our generation: the full development of self is "a process 'located' *in the core of the individual* and yet also *in the core of his communal culture,* a process which establishes, in fact, the identity of those two identities." Wharton, a self-conscious product of the old New York she recreates, had finally come to realize that the children of that time and place must forever bear its mark, cherish its values, and suffer in some degree its inadequacies. Growth, then, must proceed from an understanding of one's background—a coming to terms with one's past, not a flight from it.

—Cynthia Griffin Wolff, *A Feast of Words: The Triumph of Edith Wharton* (New York: Oxford University Press, 1977), pp. 312–13

SIDNEY H. BREMER ON SOCIAL CHANGE IN *THE AGE OF INNOCENCE*

[Sidney H. Bremer (b. 1944) is assistant professor of Urban Studies and Women's Studies at the University of Wisconsin at Green Bay, and the author of *Urban Intersections: Meetings of Life and Literature in United States Cities* (1992). Here, Bremer explores Wharton's use of metaphors and her images of stagnation and preservation to show her characters' resistance to changing social patterns.]

Structurally the novel's two-part division emphasizes the disjunction and contrasts between the urban worlds of a declining aristocracy and an upstart plutocracy. Whereas Book 1 centers its action on the private, familial scandal represented by Ellen Olenska's flight from her husband, Book II introduces the contrapuntal action of the public, financial scandal represented by Julius Beaufort's banking failure. Similarly, exclusive settings—usually the parlors, dining rooms, ballrooms, and libraries of private family residences—dominate Book I, while Newland Archer and Ellen Olenska's increasingly illicit meetings in Book II take place in unrestricted settings open to a heterogeneous public on the move—along the sidewalks, on a ferry boat, at a railroad station, and in "the congestion of carriages" where a street lamp abruptly spotlights their embrace. The contrasts spell radical change. And an awareness of its impending fulfillment informs the entire novel, which culminates in a final, retrospective chapter—when Newland Archer contrasts "the old ways" he chose when he married May Welland and "the new order" enacted by his children. The abrupt chronological gap of "nearly twenty-six years" between the penultimate chapter and the *fin du siècle* ending consigns Old New York to the remote, irretrievable past.

Stressing historical change in its postwar perspective, *The Age of Innocence* also exposes preservation—the rejection of change—as the critical flaw in Old New York's embodiment of the American myth of community. Historical skepticism, not parochial nostalgia, informs Wharton's assessment of a communalism that seeks to maintain homogeneous customs and kinship networks. She reaches through the intervening decades of history to "reconstruct—archeologically, as it were"—a lost city, as James Tuttleton has argued. But contrary to Tuttleton's interpretation of the "archeological motive" that pervades *The Age of Innocence,* Wharton's reconstruction does not reveal what "vitalized" Old New York. Instead, her controlling pattern of metaphors presents the old city's communal basis as dead and deadening. The "labyrinth" of "hieroglyphic" social forms and the "pyramid" of family connections find their full embodiment in the "funereal" banquets and "mausoleum" residence of Newland Archer's most revered relatives, the van der Luydens, who have been "rather gruesomely preserved . . . [just] as bodies caught in glaciers keep for years a rosy life-in-death." Along with the volcanically preserved matriarch of May Welland Archer's family—whose corpulence "descended on her in middle life like a flood of lava on a doomed city"—these glacial fossils dominate the "family vault" that is Old New York in *The Age of Innocence.*

As the old dream of community lives out its death in Wharton's fictional New York, moreover, any new dreams are aborted in order to preserve its mummified form. Ruled by the living dead, Old New York has an awesome power to blind the unimaginative and to bind or exile those who would dream of "other cities beyond New York." May Welland Archer represents those unimaginative young people whose veins are filled with "preserving fluid" by an insulated upbringing, transforming each into an "embodied image of the family"—by definition, resistant to change. Ellen Olenska and Newland Archer represent those other young people who gain perspective on their society's sterility by bumping up against changing realities. But they are "buried alive," prevented from enacting their perceptions, from moving beyond passive revery to an orienting vision or a new myth. Their perceptions and desires, no matter how imaginative, cannot become creative dreams, Wharton shows, if they remain unenacted—whether out of passive conformity to custom, voluntary submission to the still compelling appeal of "loyalty," or unwanted entrapment in the forms of custom that family "conspirators" join ranks to enforce. Ellen exiled, Newland apparently leads a rich, active civic life without transgressing familial bounds, but "he had missed: the flower of life," which finally became "more real" to him in fantasy than in fact. And Wharton's novel demonstrates that, to be vital, dreams must interact with the daily and historical changes of ongoing social life.

—Sidney H. Bremer, "American Dreams and American Cities in Three Post-World War I Novels," *The South Atlantic Quarterly* 79, No. 3 (Summer 1980): 276–78

CUSHING STROUT ON *THE AGE OF INNOCENCE* AS A COMPLEMENT TO HENRY JAMES'S *PORTRAIT OF A LADY*

[Cushing Strout (b. 1923) is the Ernest I. White Professor of American Studies and Humane Letters at Cornell University and the author of *The Veracious Imagination: Essays on American History, Literature, and Biography* (1981). In this extract, Strout examines the influence of Henry James on Edith Wharton, noting that Wharton's novel complements, rather than imitates, James's *Portrait of a Lady*.]

In his *Portrait of Edith Wharton* (1947) Percy Lubbock suggested that Henry James first saw her as a novel of his own, "no doubt in his earlier manner." For Lubbock he was the "master of her art" and the "master of her ceremonies" as well, whenever she visited him for one of their exhilarating tours in her car. We are led to see her as a "dazzling intruder" on the great man's solitary dedication to his art. Lubbock's memoir, almost parodically Jamesian in style and temper, ends with a vision of Wharton and James talking together as they disappear over the hill. The biographer's accolade is to say that the development of Wharton's serious literary talent has made her even more Jamesian, as if she were now a "creation of his latest manner." Wharton is engulfed in the legend of the master.

No wonder more recent admirers of Wharton have had to disassociate her from James, as she did herself from his later novels, which she found lacking in "thick nourishing human air." Irving Howe inaugurated this modern trend by arguing that since the observation of manners was only an aspect of her work, subordinated (as it was with James) to "the strength of her personal vision and the incisiveness of her mind," then it was at most only "the lesser James that influenced the lesser Mrs. Wharton." In her most important novels Howe found it hard to detect "any specific Jamesian influence." Cynthia Wolff in 1977 completed this process of severance with the purpose of establishing Wharton as a major writer in her own terms. Resonating with the women's movement's interest in reclaiming female writers, *A Feast of Words: The Triumph of Edith Wharton* decisively repudiated the patronizing older tradition of seeing her as merely a clever disciple of James.

There is an odd assumption, however, in these admirable attempts to do justice to Edith Wharton, an unintended premise that Jamesian comparisons are bound to be invidious. Moreover, the fear of linking her to James reduces the idea of influence to discipleship. I find it indicative of these tendencies that Cynthia Wolff draws back from exploring the striking relationship between James's *The Portrait of a Lady* and Wharton's *The Age of Innocence*, their two most widely read and admired works. She recognizes what she calls an "antiphonal" connection between these novels and points out that Wharton's hero (Newland Archer) and James's heroine (Isabel Archer) are further linked when a character in *The Age of Innocence* remarks that Wharton's protagonist looks like a painting, "The Portrait of a Gentleman." Moreover, Wolff knows that both novels involve issues of individual freedom and the sanctity of the marriage bond. But, in the end, the New World setting of Wharton's story, contrasted with the Old World setting of James's, and the mood of "equilibrium and acceptance" in one, contrasted with the tragic hue of the other, lead Wolff to drop the comparison as a misleading one.

The strong case for considering the two novels together goes beyond Wharton's allusions. It notices what James felt he left out of *The Portrait of a Lady*. He tells us that he pressed "least hard" on rendering the male satellites of his heroine, while focusing his attention on Isabel Archer in a way that was vulnerable to the charges of being "too exclusively psychological" and of failing to see the heroine "to the end of her situation." James felt that his book did have the unity of what "groups together," but he added that "the rest may be taken up or not, later." Because Wharton and James were close and mutually admiring friends, it is reasonable to believe that she took seriously these remarks about a work which she considered to be the perfection of his art. His observations gave her an opening for her own talent to take up "the rest" by putting the psychological in a social context, telling the male side of the story more fully, and seeing the heroine and the hero through to the end of their situation. These are the virtues, in fact, of *The Age of Innocence*, which, in this sense, complements *The Portrait of a Lady.*

To understand how it does may leave us with a clearer sense not only of their different ways of telling a story, but also of their joint interest in a moral theme. Irving Howe emphasizes their different milieux: James's ties through his theological father to New England philosophical idealism and Wharton's ties through parents and husband to "the provincial ruling class of 'old New York.'" But what justifies her reference to their common origins in "old America," whose "last traces" could be found in Europe, is, I suggest, their mutual capacity for appreciating renunciation as both a moral decision and a culturally formed trait or disposition.

—Cushing Strout, "Complimentary Portraits: James's Lady and Wharton's Age," *The Hudson Review* 35, No. 3 (Autumn 1982): 405–07

CAROL WERSHOVEN ON THE LOW NATURE OF HIGH SOCIETY IN WHARTON'S NEW YORK

[Carol Wershoven (b. 1947) coauthored with her husband a history of Florida's Gold Coast, *Boca Raton: The*

Romance of the Past (1981). She is an associate professor of English at Palm Beach Junior College. In the following extract, from her book *The Female Intruder in the Novels of Edith Wharton* (1982), Wershoven examines the hypocrisy, cruelty, and aversion to reality of "civilized" New York in *The Age of Innocence*.]

There is only a quiet irony in Ellen's belief that New York's inner goodness has made her a better person, because the result of society's passion for avoiding the unpleasant is a world filled with hypocrisy and cruelty, devoid of intellectual development.

Representative of the hypocrisy of the New York world is Lawrence Lefferts, whose marriage Archer considered to be a typical New York one, who covers up his many affairs by pontificating about the holiness of the marriage bond. Wharton increases the reader's sympathy for Ellen and anger at old New York by placing Lefferts in certain key scenes in which Ellen is being most maligned. At the farewell dinner, for example, Archer, despite his own pain, notices that "never had Lefferts so abounded in the sentiments that adorn Christian manhood and exalt the sanctity of the home," and Sillerton Jackson explains, "I hear there are pressing reasons for our friend Lawrence's diatribe: —typewriter this time, I understand." Lefferts's adultery is tolerated by New York because it is hidden, and, unlike the activities of the more open Ellen, does not threaten to disrupt the pleasurable life. It is therefore not marital fidelity that is a value in New York, but rather the appearance of it.

Similarly, although the social tribe ostensibly "exacted a limpid and impeccable honesty" in business matters, it is quite willing to accept Julius Beaufort with his disreputable past, as long as his dishonesty is kept quiet, because Beaufort gives his friends a good time. The Beauforts have a ballroom where they regularly give splendid balls, and "this undoubted superiority was felt to compensate for whatever was regrettable in the Beaufort past." Therefore, when the rumors of Beaufort's scandalous financial failure circulate, New York hopes that they are not true, for the "disappearance of the Beauforts would leave a considerable void in their compact little circle; and those who were too ignorant or too careless to shudder at the moral cata-strophe bewailed in advance the loss of the best ballroom in New York."

However, when Beaufort's empire does crash, publicly and dishonorably, New York's reaction is swift: Beaufort simply ceases to exist, socially. When his wife pleads with her kinswoman, the powerful Mrs. Manson Mingott, for support and refuge, Mrs. Mingott replies, "Honor's always been honor, and honesty honesty, in Manson Mingott's house." Mrs. Min-gott had, of course, known of Beaufort's dishonorable business methods since he had come to New York, but since his banking practices appeared to be in order, reality could be ignored. Mrs. Mingott now attempts to adhere to the same policy that had worked so well in the past: push reality away. She drives Regina Beaufort from her house and gives orders that no one should mention the Beauforts to her again. Even family members must be sacrificed so that New York will not have to look upon, or deal with, pain or dishonor.

As has already been discussed, Ellen Olenska is the most obvious victim of the cruelty of evasion. And yet the cruelty is "innocent" in a certain sense, for all the pressure applied to make Ellen return to her husband is employed without a full knowledge of what such a reconciliation would mean. Mon-sieur Rivière, the Count's secretary, explains to Archer that return to her husband would subject Ellen to certain "unthink-able" things and he is in one sense right when he says that "if Madame Olenska's relations understood what these things were, their opposition to her returning would no doubt be as unconditional as her own." But their deliberate, calculated ignorance, their refusal to hear of her sufferings, makes it morally acceptable, in their eyes, to send her back to the unthinkable, and to view her case as merely one of a woman's duty to her husband.

New York fears the real then, and this fear has many conse-quences. One of them is the elimination from society of any intellectual or creative individuals, for such persons might introduce something new and therefore dangerous into a safe environment. Society feels a "certain timidity" about artists, musicians, and writers. "They were odd, they were uncertain, they had things one didn't know about in the backgrounds of their lives and minds." Society considers it bizarre that one of their own, Emerson Sillerton, "a man who had had 'every advantage,' . . . wealth and position," should become an archaeologist, "or indeed a Professor of any sort . . . live in Newport in winter, or do any of the other revolutionary things that he did." It is not surprising, then, that Ellen can say of New York society that "except the other evening at Mrs. Struthers's, I've not met a single artist since I've been here."

While New York observed in action seems to live by no admirable values, this is not to say that *The Age of Innocence* contains no moral positives at all. The most explicit statement of values of the novel is made by Monsieur Rivière, the man rumored to have been Ellen's lover: "it's worth everything, isn't it, to keep one's intellectual liberty, not to enslave one's powers of appreciation, one's critical independence?" A person must, he says, preserve his "moral freedom, . . . one's 'quant à soi.' . . . The air of ideas is the only air worth breathing. . . . Voyezvous, monsieur, to be able to look life in the face: that's worth living in a garret for, isn't it?" This statement stands in direct opposition to the attitudes and behavior of old New York, and is a code that only one character in the novel besides Rivière himself lives by. Only Ellen Olenska can fully "look life in the face," and only she escapes from New York with her identity intact.

She is the outsider whose decency and loyalty and generosity of spirit put her critics within society to shame. Her compassion encompasses a child in the street, the outcast Regina Beaufort, and the woman her lover married in place of her. Ellen's openness and honesty enable her to share her fine, free vision with an insider, and she gives him what little he is capable of taking from her. Because Ellen has faced pain and has not run from life, she is an adult, and thus it is most fitting that Ellen be cast out of New York. As a grown-up she can find no place in a world of evasion.

—Carol Wershoven, *The Female Intruder in the Novels of Edith Wharton* (Rutherford, NJ: Fairleigh Dickinson University Press, 1982), pp. 91–93

❖

WENDY GIMBEL ON THE DIFFICULT MORAL CHOICES OF NEWLAND ARCHER AND ELLEN OLENSKA

[Wendy Gimbel teaches at Fordham University in New York City. She is presently working on a biography of Annie Adams Fields, a 19th-century Bostonian writer. In the following extract, taken from *Edith Wharton: Orphancy and Survival* (1984), Gimbel explores the significance of Dallas and Newland Archer's visit to Ellen Olenska in the book's final chapter.]

With Newland's decision to accompany his son, Dallas, to Paris, the novel moves toward a consideration of Ellen's chosen home. The heroine's initiatory journey from Mrs. Mingott's townhouse, through the Twenty-third Street rental, to the unseen Washington house of exile, ends in the "central splendour" of her flat in the Rue de Varenne. Each structure expresses the heroine's shifting perceptual relationship to the world. The final house presents an image of Ellen in her maturity.

Paris, as recreated in Newland's imagination, has long become the word for his romantic sense of Ellen. Alone, in his library, he had evoked its "radiant outbreak of spring . . . the whiff of lilacs from the flower carts, the majestic roll of the river under the great bridges." As he had envisaged the city, it could not possibly reflect the quality of Ellen's actual existence. Now, as he stands in front of her house, the concreteness of the structure and the accuracy of his historical memory play with each other to produce an emotionally resonant image of her life.

The quartier in which it sits tell[s] something of the uprooted American heroine; like Ellen, it is "quiet," despite "its splendour and its history." The building itself is "modern," a contemporary structure "without distinctive character but many-windowed and pleasantly balconied up its wide cream-colored front." Its atmosphere recalls the house of Mrs. Mingott; it is colored in the same beige tones, and equally welcoming of the world. Newland's recollection of the events in Ellen's past provides an emotional rationale for the resemblance between the two structures. As Mrs. Mingott had cared for her orphaned grandchild, so Ellen had "mothered" Fanny, the child of the late Julius Beaufort and his second wife, Fanny Ring. Ellen's maternal role in Fanny's life suggests that she has lived out her life in agreement with the female values first imagined in Mrs. Mingott. Her departure from New York, the break with Newland, came with May's announcement that she was pregnant with Dallas. In deference to the social values upon which the family is built, Ellen had left for Paris. As that choice established Ellen as an independent and caring female, it released similar energies in Newland. The feminine in himself has been realized in his total commitment to May and to their children.

The announced engagement between Fanny and Dallas transmutes the private sacrifice of Newland and Ellen into a socially redemptive act. In having cared for these children instead of for their own desires, Newland and Ellen have assumed the burden of maturity. The joyous existence of Dallas and Fanny celebrates the rightness of the choice as their marriage confirms the ongoingness of the love between Ellen and Newland. Both the library and the house suggest the achievement of that harmony between imagination and structure which Wharton believes to result from a successful coming of age.

—Wendy Gimbel, Edith Wharton: Orphancy and Survival; Landmark Dissertations in Women's Studies Series (New York: Praeger, 1984), pp. 165–66

SUSAN GOODMAN ON NEWLAND ARCHER'S LIMITED VISION

[Susan Goodman (b. 1951) is a professor of English at the University of Delaware and a literary scholar of Edith Wharton and Ellen Glasgow. She is the author of two books on Edith Wharton, including *Edith Wharton's Women: Friends and Rivals* (1990), from which the following is extracted. Goodman interprets Archer's inability to see May and Ellen as real people to society's "failure" of "effort and creativity."]

Archer thinks that "by merely raising his eyes" he can see his wife, but the slight action is indicative of how little effort he makes throughout the novel to understand or truly perceive her. He has, for example, missed the meaning of each angry stab that demands an answer. He has persistently refused to analyze the invisible claws that clasped May as soon as she accepted his betrothal sapphire and that are now beginning to lock him within their grasp. For him, "it was less trouble to conform with the tradition and treat May exactly as all his friends treated their wives than to try to put into practice the theories with which his untrammeled bachelorhood had dallied." Archer prefers to see her as a type rather than as an individual, and the picture of her at her work-frame is another in a long tradition of women immortalized doing similar handiwork. He commits the identical error with Ellen, perceiving her in turn as "the foreign adventurer," "the wronged wife," "the true love." This failure of both effort and creativity within accepted forms is what differentiates him from Ellen, makes his life predictable, and leaves him at the novel's end little changed from the young dilettante for whom "thinking over a pleasure to come often gave . . . a subtler satisfaction than its realization."

It also explains the inherent egoism in his decision to retain memories of Ellen of which he is the sole author. Ellen functions more as a symbol for his struggling "self" than as a flesh-and-blood person, and his interactions with her are another form of his interactions with May, "hieroglyphic" dialogue composed of "arbitrary signs," pauses, and silences. Archer's misreading of those signs, his "resolute determination to carry to its utmost limit that ritual of ignoring the 'unpleasant'," leads him mistakenly to assume that Ellen was guilty of adultery. That assumption determines the advice he gives her and his future. When Ellen tells Archer that they don't speak the same language, she knows that the topics and the openness of their speech, which includes words such as "adultery" and "mistress," do not disguise the fact that he never really hears her need for the values that he is preparing to cast aside.

Wharton's real target is not Archer, though. It is the society that insists on treating its women as children even after marriage has supposedly plunged them into the real business of living.

For there to be an age of innocence, fire cannot be ice and vice versa, yet May and Ellen are more alike than Archer suspects. After all, both are granddaughters of "Catherine the Great" and possess to some extent her sexuality, "strength of will," "hardness of heart, and a kind of haughty effrontery that was somehow justified by the extreme tendency and dignity of her private life." The cousins' last "long, good" talk brings them to a closer understanding of each other and of Archer's dilemma. Underlying their mutual desire to protect Archer from himself is the assumption that he could not escape becoming the prisoner of a hackneyed vocabulary. Adultery is adultery, and the individual case does not mitigate that act.

—Susan Goodman, *Edith Wharton's Women: Friends and Rivals* (Hanover, NH: Hanover University Press of New England, 1990), pp. 98–99

DAVID HOLBROOK ON NEWLAND ARCHER AND PASSION IN *THE AGE OF INNOCENCE*

[David Holbrook (b. 1923) is an author and prominent literary critic. He is an Emeritus Fellow of Downing College, Cambridge. His critical works include *Where D. H. Lawrence Was Wrong About Women* (1992) and *Charles Dickens and the Image of Woman* (1993). In an extract from his critical work on Edith Wharton, Holbrook comments on the author's skillful rendering of passion in *The Age of Innocence*.]

Newland continues to believe that "presently" it would be his task to "take the bandage from this young woman's eyes" and "bid her look forth on the world." But he recalls the Kentucky cave-fish, and how they ceased to develop eyes because they had no use for them: "What if, when he had bidden May

Welland to open hers, they could only look out blankly at blankness?" The self delusion of his confidence in assuming himself to be such a liberator is made clear, step by step, as he hovers between turning sullen about the niceties of whom Ellen Olenska may call on and feeling distress over the possibility of being asked to advise on her divorce: he hates divorce. He feels a "wave of compassion" for his cousin and believes he must save her "at all costs from further wounding herself in her mad plunges against fate."

He ponders his own mortality, and asks, "Are we only Pharisees after all?" He is "puzzled by the efforts to reconcile his instinctive disgust at human vileness with his equally instinctive pity for human frailty." He ponders his affair with "poor, silly" Mrs. Rushworth, who had been attracted by the secrecy and peril of the liaison as much as by his charm; he had emerged from it "with an undisturbed belief in *the abysmal distinction between the woman one loved and respected and those one enjoyed—and pitied*" (my italics). In this view he had been abetted by his female relatives who shared the belief that when "such things happened" it was "undoubtedly foolish of the man, but *somehow always criminal of the woman*" (my italics).

He is aware of the difference between the Anglo-Saxon, Protestant, position over such matters, and of what tended to happen in "rich and idle and ornamental societies" such as those in Europe, where a woman might be drawn into "a tie inexcusable by conventional standards" by "force of circumstances."

So, Archer is firmly embedded in conventional (chauvinistic, as we would call them today) views, and when discussing divorce with Ellen, he finds her saying to him, "But my freedom—is that nothing?" Yet she is pliable, and agrees with him: "Very well; I will do what you wish." She is persuaded into the New York view of what is fair and just. Beneath the surface, Newland Archer is more drawn to Ellen Olenska than he is conscious of, while she is attracted to him and aware of the seductive influence she exerts over him: by her sudden reference to the two occasions on which he has sent her roses, she causes in him an "agitated pleasure"; her colour rises "reluctantly and duskily" and she asks, "What do you do while May is away?"— a question that "faintly annoys" him.

Ellen runs away and sends him a note: he thinks, "what has Madame Olenska been running away from, and why did she feel the need to be safe?" It seems clear she is falling in love with Archer; she tells him, "I can't feel unhappy when you're here," and "I live in the moment when I'm happy": "The words stole through him like a temptation . . . Archer's heart was beating insubordinately. What if it were from him that she had been running away . . ." She anticipates her "stealing up behind him to throw her light arms about his neck," but Beaufort arrives—the vulgar rich adventurer who is pursuing Ellen.

Again we may reflect on the degree to which Edith Wharton has the advantage over Henry James. She knows how passionate need can creep up on a man or a woman unawares, as James did not, despite his interest in the morality of passion. She is aware of the subtleties of feminine intuition: for example, when May Welland, by a supreme effort, detects how differently Newland Archer has behaved to her since the announcement of their engagement, which happened to coincide with his interest in Ellen Olenska. May deduces that it is because of his regret over Mrs. Rushworth—and offers him his freedom, with tragic fortitude!

—David Holbrook, Edith Wharton and the Unsatisfactory Man
(New York: St. Martin's Press, 1991), pp. 124–25

KATHERINE JOSLIN ON THE WOMAN QUESTION

[Katherine Joslin is a literary critic and the author of a book on Edith Wharton, from which this extract was taken. Here she explores Newland Archer's conflicting desires and their reflection of a greater social ambivalence toward women in New York society.]

Initially attracted, as the other men are, to Ellen's exposed bosom, Newland quickly cools to her physical self, "conscious of a curious indifference to her bodily presence." He even mistakes a "blonde and blowsy" Blenker girl for her in a curious scene where he makes love to the wrong parasol. Later he forgets her voice, "that it was low-pitched, with a faint roughness on the consonants." When they do meet, he explains that he continually experiences her anew: *"Each time you happen to me all over again."* When she flings her arms about him and presses her lips to his, he pulls away. Physical passion, the feeling he has been trained to have for a woman, is not the source of his attraction: "A stolen kiss isn't what I want," he tells her. When he last sees her at the dinner party, a ritual marking her ouster from New York, Newland finds her face "lusterless and almost ugly" and, at the same time, loves it more than ever.

At the heart of his dilemma, although he doesn't know it, is the Woman Question. If a woman does not follow convention and her abilities and talents develop more in line with men, who is she? As Vernon Lee put it in her review of Gilman's *Women and Economics:* "We do not know what women are." If passion and sensuality do not draw the male suitor, what does? Newland Archer, for all his philosophizing about the essential equality of men and women, had never before Ellen Olenska considered the concrete possibilities of his abstractions. In the fiery reality of her presence, not the physical but the intellectual dimensions of her being, Newland must reconsider all he has been taught about women.

His vanity is served a socially correct version of maidenhood in the "young girl in white," May Welland, with a name that more than suggests youthful health and wholesomeness. As Christine Nilsson sings the Daisy Song in the opera *Faust,* May sits "slightly withdrawn," in pink modesty with her hair in "fair braids" and her youthful breasts fastened modestly in a "tulle tucker." Archer has had his sexual initiation in a lengthy and mildly agitating affair with Mrs. Thorley Rushworth; their liaison had been "a smiling, bantering, humoring, watchful, and incessant lie" that, as the double standard mandates, left her tainted and him experienced. Watching his fiancée at the opera, he is excited by her purity and proud of her innocence as his possession:

> "The darling!" thought Newland Archer, his glance flitting back
> to the young girl with the lilies-of-the-valley. "She doesn't even

guess what it's all about." And he contemplated her absorbed young face with a thrill of possessorship in which pride in his own masculine initiation was mingled with a tender reverence for her abysmal purity. "We'll read Faust together . . . by the Italian lakes . . ." he thought, somewhat hazily confusing the scene of his projected honeymoon with the masterpieces of literature which it would be his manly privilege to reveal to his bride.

His smug male vanity over his supposedly superior social and intellectual position will not go unpunished in the novel.

In the first few pages, Wharton's narrator explains to the reader Newland's ambivalence. His vanity desires two conflicting attributes in his future wife: the innocence of the ingenuous and sexually naïve May Welland and the experience of the "world-wise" and sexually accommodating Mrs. Thorley Rushworth. "How this miracle of fire and ice was to be created, and to sustain itself in a harsh world, he had never taken the time to think out," the narrator explains, using the dominant and conflicting imagery of the novel. "Some say the world will end in fire," Robert Frost put it, "Some say ice." Newland finds in May Welland that fire and ice in such close proximity lose their power. After marrying and living with his Diana-like May, Newland begins to feel the results: "He was weary of living in a perpetual tepid honeymoon, without the temperature of passion yet with all its exaction." The lesson the hero learns in the novel is that what he thought was manly experience turns out in the end to have been boyish innocence.

As the liberal intellectual he fancies himself to be, our hero is a portrait of an "armchair" feminist. He begins to contemplate radical ideas of sexual equality during the homosocial male rite of smoking cigars after dinner in the library. He argues with the gossiping, priggish Sillerton Jackson over Ellen Olenska's indiscretion with M. Rivière: she has apparently lived with him for a year. Aggravated already by the impression Ellen has made on him, Newland defends her right to live with whomever she chooses: "I'm sick of the hypocrisy that would bury alive a woman at her age if her husband prefers to live with harlots." He seems not to understand his own hypocrisy: if women should be free to have sexual affairs when they choose, why does he refer to the other women as "harlots"? Why, we might also ask, the qualifier "at her age"? Or why should she be free only if her husband fails to be monogamous? Archer, however, skims the surface.

—Katherine Joslin, *Edith Wharton* (New York: St. Martin's Press, 1991), pp. 97–99

KATHY A. FEDORKO ON GOTHIC ELEMENTS IN *THE AGE OF INNOCENCE*

[Kathy A. Fedorko is a literary critic and author. Among her publications is *Gender and the Gothic in the Fiction of Edith Wharton* (1995), from which this extract was taken.]

The more intensely Newland desires Ellen, the more intensely he feels himself "beyond" the life he has lived and the self he once was. "I *am* dead—" he imagines himself saying to May when he experiences the claustrophobia of their life together. "I've been dead for months and months." When he and Ellen decide to consummate their love, Newland looks at the familiar objects in his house "as if he viewed them from the other side of the grave." Aptly, this decision is made in the antiquities section of the Metropolitan Museum, where the guard walks listlessly by like "a ghost stalking through a necropolis" and vanishes down "a vista of mummies and sarcophagi" and where the shelves hold small broken objects of domesticity, for both Ellen and Newland are in an emotional world that is, as Wharton explained her own affair, "*on the hither side.*"

Though Newland realizes, because of his love for Ellen, the soul-crushing limitations of his life in old New York society with a wife he only marginally loves, he remains a captive of the system he represents. He feels both horrified and imprisoned by his realization that Ellen has been persuaded by his wife to return to Europe and that he must, at a family dinner, cordially celebrate her leave-taking ⟨. . .⟩ Newland feels himself "assisting at the scene in a state of odd imponderability, as if he floated somewhere between chandelier and ceiling"; it comes over him "in a vast flash made up of many broken gleams," that his family has presumed he and Ellen are lovers who must be separated. The deadly power of the social elite he has been part of, "the way of people who dreaded scandal more than disease, who placed decency above courage," makes him feel like "a prisoner in the centre of an armed camp."

The Gothic language suits Newland's intense sensitivity to the nuances of his plight, that he is losing what he knows he wants in his life and that he is paralyzed by the system's power: "a deathly sense of the superiority of implication and analogy over direct action, and of silence over rash words, closed in on him like the doors of the family vault." The determined friendliness of everyone is "as if the guard of the prisoner he felt himself to be were trying to soften his captivity; and the perception increased his passionate determination to be free."

A baby keeps Newland from being free ⟨. . .⟩ Newland allows May to use [her pregnancy] as a weapon to prevent him from leaving her for Ellen ⟨. . .⟩ May represents what Mary Daly calls "feminine antifeminism," the kind of woman whose internalized "patriarchal presence" leads her to look upon women like Ellen who threaten the power structure as a threat to herself. Daly's observation that "this divisiveness among women is an extension of the duality existing within the female self" captures well the role May serves for Wharton in *The Age of Innocence* as a representative of her past discomfort with female power. May is never as unaware and innocent as Newland believes she is, and her wish to save her marriage has to be respected, but she is not the frank, passionate, creative woman Ellen is.

Ellen and Newland are feminine and masculine selves that Wharton's Gothic has helped her create, willing to face the abyss of their inner darkness and to try to act on the awareness it brings. At the same time Wharton provides enough parallels between Ellen and Newland to encourage our seeing them as a unified fe/male self. They share a mutual impatience with old New York's avoidance of the "unpleasant," an interest in literature and art, and admiration for houses that deviate from the customary style, and similar views about a woman's right to freedom. Both also express the effect of their love for one another similarly, Ellen that "I shan't be lonely now" and Newland that "he should never again feel quite alone."

—Kathy A. Fedorko, *Gender and the Gothic in the Fiction of Edith Wharton* (Tuscaloosa, AL: University of Alabama Press, 1995), pp. 97–99

❖

Books by Edith Wharton

Verses. 1878.

The Decoration of Houses (with Ogden Codman Jr.). 1897.

The Greater Inclination. 1899.

The Touchstone. 1900.

Crucial Instances. 1901.

The Valley of Decision. 1902.

Sanctuary. 1903.

The Descent of Man and Other Stories. 1904.

Italian Villas and Their Gardens. 1904.

Italian Backgrounds. 1905.

The House of Mirth. 1905.

Madame de Treymes. 1907.

The Fruit of the Tree. 1907.

The Hermit and the Wild Woman and Other Stories. 1908.

A Motor-Flight Through France. 1908.

Artemis to Actaeon and Other Verse. 1909.

Tales of Men and Ghosts. 1910.

Ethan Frome. 1911.

The Reef. 1912.

The Custom of the Country. 1913.

Fighting France, from Dunkerque to Belfort. 1915.

Xingu and Other Stories. 1916.

Summer. 1917.

The Marne. 1918.

French Ways and Their Meanings. 1919.

In Morocco. 1920.

The Age of Innocence. 1920.

The Glimpses of the Moon. 1922.

A Son at the Front. 1923.

Old New York. 1924. 4 vols.

The Mother's Recompense. 1925.

The Writing of Fiction. 1925.

Here and Beyond. 1926.

Twelve Poems. 1926.

Twilight Sleep. 1927.

The Children. 1928.

Hudson River Bracketed. 1929.

Certain People. 1930.

The Gods Arrive. 1932.

Human Nature. 1933.

A Backward Glance. 1934.

The World Over. 1936.

Ghosts. 1937.

The Buccaneers. 1938.

Eternal Passion in English Poetry
   (editor; with Robert Norton). 1939.

Roman Fever and Other Stories. 1964.

Collected Short Stories. Ed. R. W. B. Lewis. 1968.

Ghost Stories. 1973.

Short Stories. 1975.

Fast and Loose. 1977.

Works About
Edith Wharton and
The Age of Innocence

Atkinson, Brooks. "Critic at Large." *New York Times* (27 March 1962): 34.

Auchincloss, Louis. *Edith Wharton: A Woman in Her Time.* New York: Viking, 1971.

Baril, James Ronald. *Vision as Metaphorical Perception in the Fiction of Edith Wharton.* Colorado: University of Colorado Press, 1969.

Bloom, Harold. *Edith Wharton.* New York: Chelsea House, 1986.

Bretshneider, Margaret Ann. *Edith Wharton: Patterns of Rejection and Denial.* Ohio: Case Western Reserve University, 1969.

Cross, Wilbur. *Edith Wharton.* New York: Appleton, 1926.

Davis, Linette. "Vulgarity and Red Blood in the Age of Innocence." *Journal of the Midwest Modern Language Association* 20 (Fall 1987): 1–8.

Doyle, Charles Clay. "Emblems of Innocence: Imagery Patterns in Wharton's *The Age of Innocence.*" *Xavier University Studies* 10, no. 2 (1971): 19–25.

Evans, Elizabeth. "Musical Allusions in *The Age of Innocence.*" *Notes on Contemporary Literature* 4, no. 3 (1974): 4–7.

Fryer, Judith. "Purity and Power in *The Age of Innocence.*" *American Literary Realism* 17 (1985): 153–68.

_____. *Felicitous Space: The Imaginative Structures of Edith Wharton and Willa Cather.* Chapel Hill: University of North Carolina Press. 1986.

Gargano, James W. *"The Age of Innocence*: Art or Artifice?" *Research Studies of Washington State University* 38 (March 1970): 22–28.

_____. "Tableaux of Renunciation: Wharton's Use of the Shaughran in *The Age of Innocence.*" *Studies in American Fiction* 15, no. 1 (Spring 1987), 1–11.

Gerould, Katharine Fullerton. *Edith Wharton: A Critical Study.* New York: Appleton, c. 1922.

Howe, Irving. *Edith Wharton: A Collection of Critical Essays.* Englewood Cliffs, NJ: Prentice-Hall, 1962.

Jacobson, Irving F. "Perception, Communication and Growth as Correlative Themes in Edith Wharton's *The Age of Innocence.*" *Agora* 2, no. 2 (1973), n. p.

Kekes, John. "The Great Guide to Human Life." *Philosophy and Literature* 8 (October 1984): n. p.

Lamar, Lillie B. "Edith Wharton's Foreknowledge in *The Age of Innocence.*" *Texas Studies in Literature and Language* 8 (Fall 1966): 85–89.

Lawson, Richard H. *Edith Wharton.* New York: Ungar, 1977.

_____. *Edith Wharton and German Literature.* Bonn: Bouvier Verlag Herbert Grundmann, 1974.

Lewis, R. W. B. *Edith Wharton: A Biography.* New York: Harper and Row, 1975.

Lindberg, Gary H. *Edith Wharton and the Novel of Manners.* Charlottesville: University Press of Virginia, 1975.

Lively, Penelope. Introduction to *The Age of Innocence.* London: Virago, 1988.

Lubbock, Percy. *Portrait of Edith Wharton.* New York: Appleton-Century-Crofts, 1947.

Lyde, Marilyn Jones. *Edith Wharton: Convention and Morality in the Work of a Novelist.* Norman: University of Oklahoma Press, 1959.

Nathan, Rhoda. "Ward McAllister: Beau Nash of *The Age of Innocence*." *College Literature* 14, no. 3 (1987): 276–84.

Price, Alan. "The Composition of Edith Wharton's *The Age of Innocence*," *Yale University Library Gazette* 55 (1980): 22–30.

Quinn, Arthur Hobson. *Edith Wharton*. New York: Appleton-Century, 1938.

Review of *The Age of Innocence*. *Spectator* 126 (8 January 1921): 55–56.

Robinson, James A. "Psychological Determinism in *The Age of Innocence*." *Markham Review* 5 (1975): 1–5.

Saunders, Judith P. "Becoming the Mask: Edith Wharton's Ingenues." *Massachusetts Studies in English* 8, no. 4 (1982): 33–39.

Smith, Grace Kellogg Shaw. *The Two Lives of Edith Wharton: The Woman and Her Work*. New York: Appleton-Century, 1965.

Strout, Cushing. "Complementary Portraits: James's Lady and Wharton's Age," *The Hudson Review* 35, no. 3 (Summer 1982): 405–15.

"*The Age of Innocence*." *Times Literary Supplement* (25 November 1920): 775.

Walton, Geoffrey. *Edith Wharton: A Critical Interpretation*. Rutherford: Fairleigh Dickinson University Press, 1970.

Wolff, Cynthia Griffin. "*The Age of Innocence*: Wharton's Portrait of a Gentleman." *Southern Review* 12 (1976): 640–58.

Index of
Themes and Ideas